IMAGES OF ENGLAND

NORWICH
STREETS

IMAGES OF ENGLAND

NORWICH STREETS

BARRY PARDUE

TEMPUS

Dedicated to my wife Carol for her patience
and to my Norwich-born son David for his encouragement.

First published 2005

Tempus Publishing Limited
The Mill, Brimscombe Port,
Stroud, Gloucestershire, GL5 2QG

© Barry Pardue 2005

The right of Barry Pardue to be identified as the Author of this work
has been asserted in accordance with the Copyrights, Designs
and Patents Act 1988.

British Library Cataloguing in Publication Data.
A catalogue record for this book is available from the British Library.

ISBN 0 7524 3505 1
Typesetting and origination by Tempus Publishing Limited
Printed in Great Britain

Contents

Acknowledgements

My grateful thanks are extended to the following people, as this book would not have been possible without their help: Clare Agate, Senior Librarian at the Norfolk and Norwich Millennium Library, and all her staff; Norfolk and Norwich County Councils; Paul Cavill, research fellow at the University of Nottingham; the English Place Names Society for *Norwich Past and Present*; Sutton Publishing and Neil Storey; Maurice Morson; George Nobbs; Hamilton Wood; Fort Publishing and Pamela Brooks; Larks Press and Richard Lane; Jarrolds Publishing; Terence Dalton Ltd and George Plunkett; J. Wentworth Day; Dorothy Cole, Master of the Great Hospital; Hodder and Stoughton and Geo W. Crutchley; the librarian at Eastern Counties Press; Barbara Wortley at Bungay.

Every endeavour has been made to contact the copyright owners of extracts and material used in this book. If anyone has been missed, this was not intended or deliberate.

Introduction

There is no doubt that Norwich is the capital and cathedral city of Norfolk. However, residents of Caister often remind us that their town was the site of an Iceni city in Roman times and is the original county capital. William White backed this up in 1845 when he quoted 'Caistor was a city when Norwich was none/and Norwich was built with Caistor stone'. Nevertheless, for this book we will settle on the view that Norwich was formed by the coming together of four or five settlements on the River Wensum. Some say that it was called Norwich because it was situated to the north of three settlements with the suffix -wich or -wick: Ipswich, Dunwich and Westwick.

An aerial view of Norwich, using as a boundary its medieval wall and the River Wensum on its eastern side, would show the city as being heart-shaped. This book shows how the streets of Norwich have always been its arteries, bringing pulsating life and nourishment to the city.

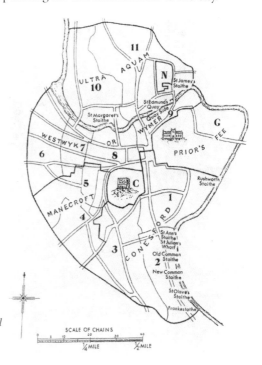

An early map of the city of Norwich, showing the medieval leets and subleets, as indicated in the Leet Roll of 1288. Also included are the locations of eleven staithes.

The origins of some street names can be clearly seen, even before looking at historical documents. For instance, Stonegate – the early name of Upper Goat Lane – may refer to the chalk and flint mines that now lie under Norwich, a city that has fabulous examples of rough and knapped flint on so many buildings. Bank Plain, Castle Hill, Cattle Market and Theatre Street are straightforward enough. Red Lion, Rose Lane and Ten Bells are all based on the names of ancient inns. Weavers Lane and Maddermarket are reminders of the medieval textile industry. Many streets take their names from churches, which are often called after saints. Some streets are named after sinners; for instance, Davey Place is a reminder of a man who once threatened to kill the King. Prominent citizens and artists like Crome and Ninham are also perpetually remembered in this way.

A number of the streets selected for this book have been chosen because they reflect the rich and varied lives of their inhabitants, whether living in poverty or wealth. Inevitably the stories also contain humour and horror not easily found in the normal archives of research.

Only fragments of the flint wall which used to enclose the city are still visible. Originally it bounded a city that was a mile and a half in length from north to south and a mile and a quarter wide from east to west. The wall once contained forty towers and twelve gates but very few remain to this day. The towers were advance-warning posts and over the centuries they were put to various uses, such as for defence and as prisons. Those near the Wensum were used as bases for levying river tolls.

Many streets led to dykes, quays, cockies and creeks and were used to transport waterborne cargoes, both legal and illegal, into the city. Smugglers were very active and led a dangerous and risky life that often finished on the gallows. The smaller watercourses were at times full of deposited refuse and sewage from outside water closets. The current in the Wensum and its tributaries was notoriously slow, so pollution was inevitable.

This book is full of snapshots and snippets of information that readers will quickly identify with. Norwich has seen many changes. The great manufacturing empires of chocolate-making, weaving, shoemaking and brewing are long gone. We still have Colmans, Norwich Union and Jarrolds but only the latter is still owned by the original family. Riots, the invention of steam trains, damage caused by the Second World War and the freedom given to architects have all played a part in taking away portions of historic Norwich streets but there are still enough left to walk through and admire. These streets provide an insight into the city's history and a comparison between the past and present. It is still easy to imagine the streets filled with busy carrier's carts, livestock drovers, farmers and gentlemen with their fashionable ladies.

If the writer George Borrow were around today, he would still call Norwich a fine city. Not because we are lucky enough to have the 'old castle upon the top of that mighty mound' or 'that cloud-encircled cathedral spire' but simply because the city has retained so many of its plains and gardens and the refurbishment of many factories, warehouses and even old inns has been completed with reasonable care. There are huge developments underway between Chapelfield East and St Stephens and also along stretches of the River Wensum. It is hoped that, when finished, these will have taken into account the valuable heritage of the city's past.

A selection of modern street names has been added to this reconstructed map of Norwich, dated 1348.

The author confesses to having a sweet tooth but this is not the only reason for including a brief history of Caley and Mackintosh: the men who owned the company were both religious men, devoted citizens and public benefactors who were beloved by their employees and fellow townsmen. They looked after their staff, both in and out of the workplace, as did J. Colman, whose products were at the opposite end of the taste spectrum.

Considerable space has been given in this book to Carrow Road and its importance, including the beneficial effect that the football club and its well-known supporter Delia Smith has had on the city. There is also reference to the Norwich canary, a bird that the football club has taken as its logo. The sweet-singing little yellow bird is known throughout the world as a benchmark of quality and is the highest standard that canary breeders aim for.

The history of the city is visible in many of the streets of Norwich, especially those which were enclosed by the medieval walls. The surface of their history has only been scratched within this book, which does not profess to be an archaeological document. It is hoped that the book will spur the interest of the reader to investigate further and become 'streetwise' and more fully able to appreciate the events that have shaped the city over the past 1,300 years. The city has seen invasions and sackings by the Danes, the building of the churches and castles, the establishment of friaries, the Black Death, charters and guilds, rebellions, the arrival of 'strangers' and Flemish weavers, royal visits, wars and industrial development. Evidence of the past is there for all to see in the streets and their place in the history of Norwich is ongoing.

A

Agricultural Hall Plain

This was originally called Castle Meadow although another street now carries the name. It was a steep hill that formed part of the defences of Norwich Castle and is close to the upper part of Prince of Wales Road. The imposing structure of Agricultural Hall dates back to 1882; it was opened by Prince Edward, which shows how important the city was as a centre for the farmers of Norfolk. In those days, the hall's spacious interior and perimeters would have been crowded with livestock, forming queues that extended all the way around Castle Mound. It was later used for every type of entertainment, including circuses, plays, roller-skating, military tattoos and political speeches. Its neighbour, Hardwick House, is a grand neoclassical building that was once Harvey and Hudson's Crown Bank, which opened in 1866 and closed four years later. The building later housed the main post office. Both Agricultural Hall and Hardwick House are currently the home of Anglia Television.

Agricultural Hall Plain, looking towards Prince of Wales Road.

A recent picture looking down Prince of Wales Road.

All Saints Green

In its time this street has had different names, some of which were rather amusing. It was once Lame Dog Lane and was called Swynemarket for a time, before the pig trade was moved to Orford Hill in the thirteenth century. Another of its names was Brazen Door Lane; the brazen or iron door was a gate into the city that was not large enough for carriages to enter. The gate was widened in 1726 but only lasted for another sixty-six years.

This busy thoroughfare ran from Queens Road to All Saints church, which once had a thatched roof. The street takes its name from the church; the 'Green' comes from the small area of land in front of the church. An alley runs between the church and the old Deacons Bank, which was called another amusing name: The Barking Dickey (*see* Westlegate). The Carlton cinema, which became the Gaumont and is now a bingo hall like a lot of old picture houses, is on the old Swynemarket land.

The sometimes outrageous writer, actor and comedian, Stephen Fry, spent a lot of his childhood in Norfolk and recalls seeing *The Great Race* in the Gaumont cinema when he was eight years old. Later on, he had difficulty getting into the City College but his cheek and his confident prediction that he would definitely get A and S levels, convinced the college to let him in. He went on to win a scholarship to Queen's College, Cambridge. In 1997, the University of East Anglia awarded him an honorary Doctorate of Letters at the same time as Salman Rushdie.

Fry is a regular supporter of the Norwich City football club. In 2002, when he learned that the club was struggling financially, he put his money where his mouth was and bought some shares, stating that it was 'a wonderful opportunity to be able to support a club that you love, by buying shares at whatever

Left: *The Carlton cinema at night. It became the Gaumont cinema, where an eight-year-old Stephen Fry saw* The Great Race.

Opposite: *This building is a fine legacy left by Barclays Bank.*

level'. Stephen Fry is a Norwich rebel and throughout his life he has been dogged with personal and corporate battles. When he was fourteen he used his father's pipe to smoke tea as he'd heard that 'it gave you a buzz'; whether it did or not, it never deterred him from smoking for the rest of his life. In 2003, he received the Pipe Smoker of the Year award from the Pipe Smokers' Council. Delighted to win this award, he said, 'I am the most famous puffer in Britain – and you can take the 'er' off that'.

B

Balderstone Court

In 1761, there was a school here for the children of poor families. Later the congregation of the Independent Meeting House met here. The street was named after Mathew Balderstone, who left money for the foundation of a charity school. There is a memorial to a Timothy Balderstone (died 1764) in St George Colegate.

Bank Plain

Originally called Motstowe, which means 'meeting place', this street has also been called Red Well Plain and Blue Boar Lane. Its current name is taken from Barclays Bank, whose premises occupied the whole of one side of the street. This monumental building was completed in 1929. Barclays have now relocated but have been trading in Norwich under different names for 200 years.

Architect George Skipper's work abounds in Norwich and one of his masterpieces is the old Royal Hotel, now an office block, that fronts onto Agricultural Plain. Its turrets and gables resemble many a tall manor or Laird's house that one sees on Scottish estates. Similar styles can be seen on what remains of the old Norfolk and Norwich Hospital in St Stephens Road.

The Royal Hotel was still open when the author first came to Norwich. It served the local delicacy of samphire, as a starter to be eaten with dressed Cromer crab. This delicious and nutritious plant grows in the salt marshes and creeks around the Norfolk coast. It tastes wonderful eaten by hand with melted butter dripping off it. Samphire has become very popular, especially in fashionable London, where even Harrods have sold it. This has put the price up and the exact location of many prime growing sites is still a closely guarded secret.

Barnards Yard

To find Barnards Yard, you have to cross Miles Bridge – built by James Frost in 1804 to replace an earlier stone bridge – to the north bank of the River Wensum. Continue a short distance up Coslany Street and on the right is Barnards Yard. Until 1976, this was the site of Barnard, Bishop & Barnard Ironworkers, who invented the first wire netting.

Barn Road

This now forms part of the Inner Ring Road and is always busy, taking traffic from Grapes Hill to Station Road. Remains of the city wall are visible here.

Left: *The Royal Hotel is another masterpiece by Norwich architect George Skipper.*

Below left: *A plate of delicious Norfolk samphire.*

Below right: *Sue and Peter Cooke picking samphire at a secret location in Norfolk. They sell it in their seafood shop at Salthouse.*

Right: *These men at the ironworks are posing in their clean clothes, which belies the dirty and harsh conditions of working here during the 1920s.*

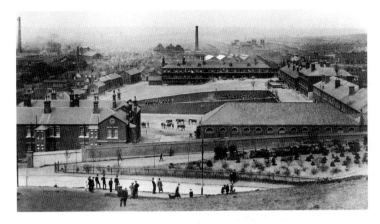

A view from the slopes of Mousehold Heath, showing the parade square and the Cavalry horses being exercised. The smoke over the city gives an indication of the amount of manufacturing industry at that time.

Barrack Street

This street runs from Peacock Street to the Ketts Hill roundabout and is now part of the Inner Ring Road. It was once a quite run-down area with slums and tenements but these were cleared in 1960 as part of a five-year demolition programme. During this time, the brewery and the Horse or Cavalry Barracks, which dated back to 1791, were taken down.

The Cavalry Barracks were the home of the Scots Greys regiment. In 1826, they were in action against a crowd of weavers who were rioting in Norwich. The weavers were destroying anything they could find that had been imported into the country for use in the textile industry and, when they started to break windows in local factories, the soldiers had to call for reinforcements. Citizens were sworn in as special constables to increase the strength of the soldiers, who were then able to quell the riot.

Four soldiers from the Cavalry Barracks were accused of murdering one of their colleagues, who was suffering from a well-known disease contracted from 'ladies of the night'. In an attempt to cure him, they went to his isolated sickroom and blocked the chimney with straw. They then closed the windows and lit plates of sulphur which were placed on the floor. This remedy killed rather than cured and he died a few days later. The understanding jury decided to acquit the soldiers, as their friend would have died anyway from the disease.

Bedford Street

Once known as Lobster Lane, this street was later named after the Bedford Arms public house, which ceased trading in the nineteenth century.

Old Post Office Yard leads off Bedford Street. In 1864, Caley's mineral water business moved here from London Street, as their original premises could not cope with their booming business. They introduced additional products such as ginger beer, tonic water, lemonade and potash. At this time in his career, Caley had no thought of making chocolate (*see* Chantry Road).

Above left: *An inside view of Ber Street gate, from J. Kirkpatrick's print of 1720.*

Above right: *Black Anna's pub, the Jolly Butchers. A favourite place for those who enjoyed live music and singing with their ale.*

Ber Street

This wide street is thought to have been an old Roman road used by soldiers en route from their camp at Caister, although some local archaeologists are not convinced. The old Ber Street gate entrance to Timber Hill was near here; it was considered to be the most important entrance to Norwich as it led directly to the castle. Unfortunately, the gate was demolished in 1726 and rebuilt using local brick that did not last. It was finally taken down completely in 1808.

There used to be an Italian community in this street, making wonderful ice cream, but they are long gone.

The street used to be known as Blood and Guts Street, a name which probably arose because cattle were driven along here to the abattoir. The name could also refer to the fights that regularly took place when the public houses closed their doors. The landlady of the Jolly Butchers was Black Anna, a great singer and a tremendous character of Italian descent. In the early nineteenth century, there was another popular but more genteel establishment called the Greyhound Inn, which had a bowling green and was the principal venue in the city for garden parties.

Bethel Street

This road runs parallel with St Giles Street – named after the Provençal hermit and popular patron saint of cripples and beggars – on the south side of City Hall, and meets up with Upper St Giles Street on the west side. It was once known as Newport Street, a name which meant 'new town' in the days of the Norman Conquest. 'Port' was often used in street names in towns with market rights; this is interesting because the city market stalls are not too far away.

A fine view of gabled houses in Bethel Street, with the tower of St Peter Mancroft in the distance.

The name Bethel comes from the Bedlam Hospital situated on the south side of the street. It was founded in memory of the late husband of Mary Chapman in 1713. The Chapmans had mentally ill relatives and this is what spurred Mary on to build a progressive new hospital for 'poor lunatics' and 'not natural born fools and idiots'. Her life was spent in compassionate work at the hospital, at a time when there were only two units in the country. She died in 1724 without ever being properly recognised for the work she had done.

There must have been plenty of people needing treatment because the hospital was enlarged on two occasions, in 1807 and 1899. In 1813, the Master of the Hospital, James Bullard, was killed by a patient at the age of sixty-seven. He died from a stomach wound inflicted with a scythe by Jonathan Morley, who was mowing the lawn. Morley was found guilty of wilful murder and sent to a newly opened criminal lunatic asylum in London. The highly respected Norwich boxer Richard Cricknell, who passed away in 1842, was a Bethel patient for two years after a head injury deprived him of reason. In those days, many lunatics were considered no better than criminals; they were figures of fun and subjected to cruel taunts.

Bethel Street was originally called Committee Street because of the proximity of Committee House but this name did not last because the whole area was blown up during a riot in 1648, in which 100 people were killed or injured.

There used to be gabled houses all along the north side of this street but they were demolished in 1938 to accommodate the new fire station and later City Hall. This was acceptable to some people but others thought that it was madness for the council planners to flatten the massive area between the hospital and Hay Hill. The planners were responsible for the abysmal buildings that one can see today.

Fortunately this street did have in its past a man with great artistic talent: John Crome, founder of the Norwich School of Painters. In 1783, he was indentured as a seven-year apprentice to Francis Whistler, a signwriter and coach-painter who lived at No. 55 Bethel Street. Crome's early days here were puritanical: he was never allowed to go to alehouses or taverns or to play any gambling games such as dice or cards. He was especially warned not to commit fornication and to keep away from 'naughty' ladies. On the plus side, he had plenty of food, clean accommodation and more than adequate clothes. He even had the services of nurses if he was unwell.

Bishopgate

This is one of the oldest streets in the city and once formed part of the original Roman road that ran from east to west before Norwich really developed. It used to be called Holme Street, the name deriving from the word for water meadow. The name Bishopgate comes from the city gate at the end of Bishops Bridge. The west end of the street, where it joins St Martins, was at one time named Tabernacle Street because of the Methodist tabernacle that was here until 1953, when it was demolished in the year of its bicentenary.

In 1999, it was the 750th anniversary of the foundation of the Great Hospital, which was once known as St Giles hospital. It was founded in 1249 by the well-loved Bishop Walter Suffield, who claimed that the establishment of the hospital was 'in remission of my sins'; such a generous act was considered an effective means of securing perpetual prayers for one's soul. After the bishop died, the population of Norwich continued to benefit from his generosity. He left money to the poor of the city, including sums for clothing, and as his coffin passed through the streets, money was handed

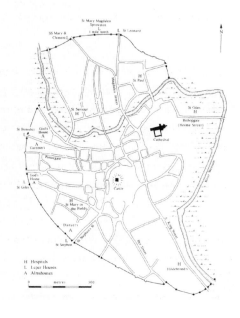

The hospitals of medieval Norwich.

The church of St Helen's and part of the old hospital.

Treatment of sore legs was a regular occurrence but intrusive surgical procedures were rare and a final resort.

to the poor who had turned out to pay their respects. All the bishop's servants were remembered by name, even the kitchen boys and chimney sweeps. His horses and pack of hounds were given to the King. The cathedral, the hospital and the friars and monks of the city all received money.

The Great Hospital was not a hospital in today's sense of the word, as medical treatment was not provided and anyone with a contagious or incurable disease was denied entry. At the beginning, it was intended as a home for poor priests, scholars and sickly people; here they were fed hot meals and given clothes and lodging in warm surroundings. Later, at least seven poor boys with good voices were chosen on merit from The Norwich School and local grammar schools. They were allowed to stay until they had a good grasp of Latin and, armed with this knowledge, many went on to become priests. The intertwined history of the hospital and The Norwich School dates back to the thirteenth century. The school choir continues to sing at St Helen's during special services. Thirteen non-resident paupers were given a meal every day that consisted of bread and fish, or meat, and ale. On occasion, they were even given cheese and eggs, which provided a welcome change of diet. In the harsh winters, the paupers were allowed inside the gates and came into the hospital to eat their meals by a warm fire. On special days, such as the Feast of the Annunciation and the Feast of St Dunstan, up to 300 meals would be served. The bishop decreed that no more than four nuns should attend to the well-being of everyone. He never allowed female residents in the hospital and the nuns were all aged over fifty because he thought that having younger ladies would encourage sexual activity.

Over the centuries, the hospital has been enlarged and modernised. It is still known as the Great Hospital and this title is very apt, for its 130 residents are well looked after by the trustees, staff and friends who provide a high level of care. The first Master of the Hospital was Hamon de Calthorpe; the current holder of this position is Dorothy Cole, the hospital's first female Master. Under her guidance, the hospital is assured of an illustrious future.

Above: *St Helen's Church. Caring for the soul was extremely important but more emphasis was placed upon treating bodily infirmities.*

Right: *One of the women's cubicles, which were not phased out until the 1980s.*

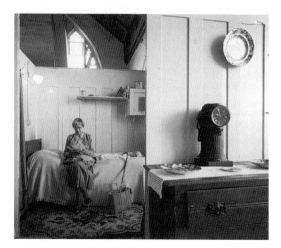

Swans were fattened at Bishopgate and sold for high prices.

The ancient church of St.Helen's has for centuries been a place of worship for the community of the hospital, which has become more well known as a collection of almshouses. When first built, the church was considered by many to be the largest and grandest in Norwich. John Everard, who was the chief mason working on the cathedral, also carried out work in this church. The creed board, which is now placed behind the altar, was used at a time when adult literacy was poor. There is a 300-year-old silver sanctuary lamp hanging before the altar and some fine medieval carving on the ends of the two front pews. On the church door is a sixteenth-century eulogy of the Tudors that makes interesting reading. Many historic moments have occurred in St Helen's church over the past 750 years, none more so than the wedding of Dorothy Cole and Revd Owen North, a United Reformed Church minister. The church was an appropriate setting for this marriage, as it was here that the Congregationalist movement joined with the Presbyterian Church of England to form the United Reformed Church. As well as being the first lady Master of the Hospital, Dorothy is the first Master to be married in St Helen's church.

Another point of interest in Bishopgate is the swan pit, which was in existence as early as 1489. It was here that swan-upping, the annual rounding-up of the swan population so that that they could be marked to indicate ownership, took place. Swans used to be considered a delicacy and the unfortunate birds were force-fed, killed and dressed for the table. They were sold for two guineas and upwards, which was a very high price in the city. More recently, cygnets were obtained from the river Yare and its Broads.

London-born artist Leslie Davenport (1908-1973), who was loved by the citizens of Norwich for his striking and unique style in paintings of the city, lived at No. 54 Bishopgate and frequented the nearby Red Lion Inn. His sixteenth-century house, now known as The Hermitage, was at one time the rectory of St-Mary-in-the-Marsh church, which no longer exists.

Bishops Bridge Road

Bishops Bridge is the only medieval bridge left in the city and is thought to date from 1340. It once belonged to the Church and was under the control of the bishop but sometime in the fourteenth century it was passed to the citizens of Norwich and was controlled by the City Corporation. There were several bridges over the River Wensum within the old city walls but this was the only bridge that gave access from outside the city. It therefore formed part of the defences of the city and had a fortified gatehouse built by a rich citizen, Richard Spynk, at his own expense. As a reward for this gesture, he and his descendants were allowed to live for all time without paying any taxes or tolls. When the City Corporation took over the bridge, they decided to rent the gatehouse out. In 1790, engineers found that the structure of the bridge was cracking under the weight of the gatehouse and it was demolished.

Criminals who had been sentenced to death at the stake were forced to walk over the bridge carrying the faggots which, when lit, would burn them alive. They were buried in Lollard's Pit, which is nearly opposite the bridge (see Llolards Road).

Furious battles took place at Bishops Bridge during Kett's Rebellion in 1549. Robert Kett was a landowner who marched on Norwich to demand justice for the poor. One bloodthirsty fight took place when some of the Earl of Warwick's troops, who were bringing in fresh ammunition and cannon, took the wrong route and met the rebels here. The rebels won the ensuing battle, took over the armaments and used them to good effect. However, the rebellion ultimately failed and Kett was hanged for treason.

Botolph Street

Once commonly called Buttle Street, this street takes its name from the Abbot of St Buttolph. A church of this name was demolished in the sixteenth century. It was situated nearer to Magdalen Street and in fact its churchyard was adjacent to that street. Henry VIII gave it to Will Godwin as private property in 1544 and it was he who let it deteriorate into a pile of rubble.

Prior to the Anglia Square modernisation, there was an ancient inn called the King's Arms here. In 1845, landlord Henry Yaxby was proud of the fact that on the gable end of his building were the letters IC and the date 1646. He would be pleased to know that these are now preserved in the Norwich Museum.

Bracondale

Bracondale now forms part of the southern section of the Inner Ring Road. Bracondale School was situated here; in 1926, the school had a bright pupil who was selected as a future teacher. He had other talents on the cricket pitch that were spotted by the school coach, who was a past county player for Lancashire. The protégé was Bill Edrich, who played for Norfolk at the age of sixteen, later played for Middlesex and then went on to have a glorious career for England.

A good example of knapped flint.

Bridewell Alley

Once known as St Andrews Lane, this is one of the oldest shopping streets in Norwich and some of the shop façades are hiding sixteenth-century timber-framed houses. The street takes its name from the Bridewell Museum situated behind the church. This fourteenth-century building, whose north side has the best example of knapped flint in England, was built by the father of William Appleyard, the first mayor of Norwich. It was turned into a prison in 1583 and may have been called after a London prison of this name situated near St Bride's Well. It continued as a prison until 1828 and was later used as a factory. In 1923, it was restored and given to the city as a museum of local trades.

In 1902, items worth £1,000 were stolen from the jewellery shop owned by Edward Hugh Briggs, including 34 gold watches, 40 gold Albert chains, 275 gold gem rings and 138 brooches, and the theft was reported in both local and national papers. The culprit was John Lane, who was staying at the Eastbourne Hotel on Rose Street. He aroused the suspicion of hotel owner Mrs Whitrod when he went to the local chapel carrying a light brown bag. The next day, as Mrs Whitrod was cleaning the sitting room, she had to move the same bag and saw a brace, bit and candle inside it. Her testimony had Lane sentenced to five years' penal servitude.

Bridge Street

This street over the River Wensum connects St Georges to Wensum Street. In 1802, the remains of the Black Friary were repaired and enlarged to form a workhouse that extended down to the river. Over 700 paupers were accommodated and those able to work were employed in the manufacture of cotton and worsted goods. The yearly cost of maintaining an inmate was £5 in today's money, at a time when the salary of the workhouse master was £70.

Brigg Street

Situated just off this street was Tolls' Court, the site of a seminary run by Miss Heazel where, in 1811, Old John Crome – father of the famous artist – was teaching drawing. At the same time, he taught this subject to the Gurney family but soon ran into their debt, owing over £200. He held a sale of his paintings, which got him out of trouble, and three years later he had nearly £1,000 in his bank account. During this period, he became drawing master at the grammar school.

Bull Close

Bull Close connects Cowgate to Bull Close Road. In the eighteenth century, this was a mass of fields and pastures that provided good grazing for cattle, and the names of these roads are a reminder of this rural activity. This productive area was bounded on two sides by Magdalen Street and Magdalen Close. Landlord Essau Pye kept the Bull Inn that stood on the corner of Bull Close and Bull Close Road.

C

Calvert Street

A large shoe factory and upholstery works was located in this street. In 1978, it was converted by the city council into flats and named Octagon Court due to the proximity of the Presbyterian Octagon chapel in Colegate.

Poet, novelist and outstanding beauty Amelia Opie was born in a house in this street in 1769. Her first novel, *Father and Daughter*, was published in 1801 and reprinted many times. Because of good looks, Opie was the star of fashionable society and on her infrequent visits to London she enjoyed the attention and affection of various admirers such as artists, writers and statesmen, including Wordsworth, Byron and the family of Napoleon.

Between Calvert Street and St George Street is a good example of a flint house, once owned by a merchant named Bacon. St George Street was once called Gildergate, a name said to refer to the fact that herring from Great Yarmouth were kippered or 'gilded' there.

In 1832, Thomas Foyson, who ran a small family vinegar works in this street, got himself in a pickle. He was overcome by fumes while gauging a vat of the liquid, fell in and was drowned, leaving a widow and nine children. The local newspapers were quite nasty in their reports, remarking on the fact that 'his life was insured for a large sum'.

Horace Booty, master of the Presbyterian School in this street, had a lucky escape on 10 September 1874. He was travelling on a train between Norwich and Brundall when, to protect his family from hearing strong language from a fellow passenger, he moved them to another carriage.

The train had a head-on collision with a mail train and their original carriage was smashed to pieces, so his courteous decision saved all their lives.

Carrow Hill

This road continues across King Street towards the River Wensum and forms part of the entrance into the Colman's factory, which is surrounded by Carrow Hill, King Street, Carrow Road and the River Wensum. The reason Colman's moved into the city from Stoke Holy Cross was to be close to the river and the railway.

J.J. Colman was to become one of the greatest citizens of Norwich: he was sheriff then mayor and was also a magistrate, an MP and the Deputy Lieutenant for Norfolk. He was given the freedom of the city in 1893 and founded the *Eastern Evening News* with a few of his friends. The mustard mill opened here in 1856 with improved working practices and equipment. At the same time, new small containers with bright yellow labels were introduced, a trademark of the company that still exists today. Royal warrants came from many different countries and Colman's were appointed mustard-makers to Queen Victoria, Napoleon III and Emmanuel II of Italy. Great success followed at the Moscow Exhibition of 1878 and Colman was even awarded the French Cross of the Legion of Honour.

The high quality of all Colman's products garnered many international awards. Their Azure Blue starch won a gold medal award in 1872 at the Moscow Exhibition, as did their mustard. Flour was also produced and this won a silver medal in the same exhibition. All these very fine products were filtered through silk that was produced in their own silkworm farms.

Colman's mustard factory, with the Black Tower on the hill to the left.

Colman thought a lot about the welfare of his employees, treating everyone as a personal friend. Religion was important to this family man, who had six children. At its height, his factory employed over 3,000 people and its premises occupied nearly twenty-seven acres; many employees had the benefit of growing their own crops on land provided by Colman. He did not believe in drinking alcohol and saw to it that all the public houses near to the factory were closed down, replacing these with a coffee house in nearby Trowse. Colman provided a school for the children of his employees and a health scheme for them and their parents. He was ahead of his time as far as staff benefits were concerned: he had the first factory nurse in the country and the first residential home for retired workers. When employees passed away, they were buried in coffins made in the factory carpentry shop. This 6ft-tall man was a giant of industry and human kindness and a politician with integrity, who turned down royal honours.

Although Colman's are now part of Unilever, they are still in business, with 200-300 workers. The world famous mustard brand in its yellow tin is as popular as ever, as are more modern items made by the company. With such a heritage, Norwich would not be the same without them.

Carrow Road

Originally built in 1817 to link Ber Street to the old Carrow Bridge, the whole layout was changed when the bridge was rebuilt and the section west of King Street was renamed Carrow Hill.

The old Carrow Bridge was built in 1810 and situated further down the river from the present bridge, which is just inside the city walls. As bridges go, the new bridge is quite a recent structure, as it opened in 1923. Funds for building and maintaining bridges did not came from revenues provided from the City Corporation; Carrow Bridge was built using money obtained by the Tonnage Committee, who placed tolls on all cargoes coming upriver. The committee had no responsibility for the roads, which would have deteriorated had the government not brought in an Act of Parliament that finally forced local authorities into carrying out road improvement schemes.

Carrow Road is now known all over the country and in other parts of the world as being the home of Norwich City football club. There are times when Norfolk fields are a mass of yellow and green from early-growing corn, barley, and oilseed rape and this may have a bearing on why the city football team has yellow and green on their strip. When Colman's were the club's sponsors, some people called the yellow 'mustard'. When the team went into the Premiership on 21 April 2004, seventy years to the day since they moved up from Division Three South, it was hard to separate the green and yellow fields from the streets of Norwich, as every house window, shop, office and vehicle had a quantity of bunting, balloons or flags. Even the sedate City Hall had a huge inflatable canary perched on its roof. The centre of the city was brought to standstill as an open-topped bus brought the team to City Hall for a civic reception. Fifty thousand people came together in a parade that was reminiscent of the expression of solidarity after the Second World War; there was even a flypast of Jaguar jets by the RAF. The prosperity and spirit of the city will be transformed by the team's success and house prices are already increasing.

The old Carrow Road closed on 23 November 1885.

A bird's eye view of the Canaries celebrations.

There is a distinct bond between the Norwich City directors, players, fans and residents of Norwich and Norfolk. Space must be given in this book to the First Lady of Norfolk, Delia Smith. For over eight years, she and husband Michael Wynn Jones have been joint majority shareholders and have kept the club afloat through difficult times. The outstanding achievement of their promotion into the Premiership reflects the support that Delia has given to the Canaries, and will improve all aspects of life in the city and the whole of East Anglia. Delia is thoroughly enjoying her role and her devotion to the club shone through during the celebrations. We can only hope that the team maintains its position in the Premier division.

It was Delia's childhood experiences which gave her an early insight into cooking. When food was rationed during the Second World War, shortages of all kinds of food in the shops prompted a lot of skilful activity in the kitchen, in order to make limited ingredients into tasty meals. Delia's

Above: *The team bus struggles through Castle Meadow.*

Left: *The First Lady of Norfolk, Delia Smith.*

parents were good cooks but it was her grandfather in particular who inspired her, showing her how to find and pick wild mushrooms, for example. The seed was sown in those early days and Norwich is reaping the benefit now. The University of East Anglia has awarded Delia an honorary Doctor of Letters. Perhaps she will take on the job of mayor, which would certainly go down well with everyone in the city and the county, for people who know her or have had contact with her are well aware that Delia is not slow in expressing her views 'straight from the hip'.

Castle Hill

The castle gallows once stood here. William Calcraft carried out the last public execution in Norwich in 1867 when prisoner Hubbard Lingley, aged twenty-two, was dispatched in front of the many thousands who had crowded onto the hill. The hands of those killed on the gallows were said to have mystical charms in helping to cure barrenness in women and afflictions of the neck and throat and it was not unknown for women to attempt to get below the gallows, or to convince the hangman by many devious flirtatious means to let them get close to the body, so that they could get a fresh brush of the hand of the executed before it had gone cold.

The largest animal market in the eastern counties was held here every Saturday, with people trading in sheep, cattle and horses. It was on this hill, amid the clamour and noise from the gypsies and horse dealers, that author George Borrow was moved to write, in *Lavengro*, of a wonderful old horse named Old Marshland Shales.

> So it came to pass that I stood on Castle Hill observing a fair of horses... An old man draws nigh: he is mounted on a lean pony, and leads by the bridle one of these animals... smaller than the rest and gentle, which they are not... his action differs from all the rest... he advances, the clamour is hushed... people are taking off their hats... surely not to that steed?... Yes verily!... 'What horse is that?' said I to a very old fellow... 'The best in Mother England... if you should chance to reach my years you may boast to thy grandboys thou has seen Marshland Shales'.

This creature was the greatest horse ever to set hoof on Norfolk soil. Bred from a mare called Hue and Cry, he was born nearly 200 years ago in an archway under the altar of the church of Walpole St Peter. The church is known as 'the gem of Marshland churches', hence the name of the horse.

A macabre way of curing ailments in women, especially barrenness.

Borrow's writings remind us that Norwich in those days was not only a centre of industry, manufacturing mustard, iron, steel, beer, shoes and linen, or a city full of bishops, monks, artists and merchant bankers. There were also herds of sheep, bullocks, horses and pigs, bringing the sights, sounds and smells of the countryside right into the city. Pubs drew their own particular and varied clientele from businessmen, farmers, drovers, equipment drivers, marshmen and thatchers; all had their favourite places of refreshment where they could talk or just mardle.

From the vantage point of Castle Hill in the calm of night, it is possible even now to sense that you are close to the countryside. In the stillness of the dark, under the stars, you can hear flocks of wild geese flying and calling overhead.

Castle Meadow

Not to be confused with the actual castle meadow, which was situated where Agricultural Hall Plain now stands, Castle Meadow is the name of a thoroughfare running from Orford Place to Agricultural Hall Plain. Once a very narrow road, it became a busy tram route and the 'clanking monsters', as they were known, created fear among the less agile, who had to negotiate a very narrow pavement between the tramlines and an iron railing protecting the castle gardens (see King Street).

The shops along this street have never been of great architectural interest but it is worth mentioning that the first shop in Norwich to sell wireless equipment, E & C Gates Ltd, was located here. For under £40, a unit could be purchased from Gates that would receive morse code through headphones. Things are a bit different now: we are bombarded with music from shops, pubs, street musicians and cars that can be heard from miles away because their radios are at full volume.

The exact origins of Norwich Castle is a cause of heated debates amongst historians. However, it is thought that Norwich had a royal castle built on a trench raised by Uffa in 642 for King Anna of the East Angles. Uffa later gave it as a wedding gift to his daughter Ethelfreda when she married

A noisy but effective mode of transport.

Tombert, a noble Fenmen from Lincolnshire. In Roman times, it was called Venta Icenorum and was protected in the south by Ad Tavum, a fort at Tasburgh, and even bigger garrisons housed in forts at Caister and Burgh Castle. Because of its location, which commands extensive views over the surrounding countryside, many battles have taken place between contending parties for its occupancy. In 1075, it became the only royal palace in Norfolk and Suffolk. Ralph of Wader – the Earl of Norfolk and Suffolk at that time – was its first constable, holding it for the king. There is a similarity between Norwich Castle and Castle Rising near Kings Lynn, mainly in the location of the internal rooms that were often a place of refuge, accessible only by a staircase.

The floor of the great hall is higher than that of the keep basement, which is a dismal place lit only through narrow slit windows. Archers could be placed at the windows; they were able to communicate with each other through small tunnels between each window. Pillars that supported a floor on the same level as the present gallery can be seen on the north side of the basement and there is also a deep well. Dungeons where prisoners were kept are only just below the floor of the castle and on the walls are unusual scratchings attributed to them. Prisoners were not tortured here but they were made to work extremely hard, grinding corn on treadmills. The same method was used to pump water from springs under the castle and this went on until the early nineteenth century. Public executions took place on the gatehouses until 1867; after that they were carried out inside the castle.

The clinical but attractive building we recognise today was resurfaced with Bath sandstone and limestone in 1837 and contains the Castle Museum, opened by the Duke of York (later King George V) in 1894. It has remarkable and interesting natural history collections and local antiquities, and a picture gallery which has examples of the famous Norwich School, including Old Crome, Cotman, Stark, and Vincent. Other popular Norfolk artists such as A.J. Munnings and Arnesby Brown are also well represented. The castle was refurbished in 2001 at a cost of £11.8 million and is now right up to date. There are interactive displays and parts of the castle, to which the public did not previously have access, which have now been opened up.

The attractive castle building was resurfaced with Bath sandstone and limestone in 1837. It contains the Castle Museum.

Cathedral Close – Upper and Lower

Norwich Cathedral is a gem of architectural beauty. Its history goes back to 669, when Bishop Bisi found that his diocese was too large and divided it into two parts. The original see was at Dunwich and the second at North Elmham. In the ninth century, the see was reunited at North Elmham. In 1070, Bishop Herfast, William the Conqueror's chaplain, moved the see to Theford; Bishop Herbert de Losinga moved it to Norwich in 1091.

There are two entrances to the cathedral from Tombland, through either the Erpingham or Ethelbert Gates, both of which lead to the precincts. The Ethelbert Gate was constructed in 1275 using money obtained from the residents of Norwich after they fell out with the monks. It has a chamber above the arch that was originally a chapel to St Ethelbert. The Erpingham Gate was built in 1420 by Sir Thomas Erpingham, immortalised as a warrior by Shakespeare in *Henry V* and

Below left: *The thirteenth-century Ethelbert Gate is the earliest of the two entrances to the cathedral precincts from Tombland.*

Below right: *The kneeling figure of warrior Sir Thomas Erpingham is in the niche above the arch of the gate named after him.*

Norfolk's favourite son, Lord Nelson, attended the grammar school, which is next door to the chapel of St John, built in around 1318.

a great hero of the county, and indeed the country, having fought all over the world. The gate's high porch contains many statues in small niches. One is of a kneeling figure that is supposed to be Sir Thomas with his coat of arms and representations of his two wives.

After passing through the Erpingham Gate, the grammar school is on the left. The school has a chapel of St John, built in around 1318 by Bishop Salmon. Famous scholars include Lord Nelson; Sir James Brooke, Rajah of Sarawak; Dr Martineau and George Borrow. There is a statue of Nelson opposite the school.

The cathedral's choir, tower and 315ft-high spire – believed to be the second highest in the country – dominate all other buildings around it. On entering the cathedral, the grace and beauty of the soaring interior takes your breath away. The nave is 70ft high and is full of carvings of men, women, angels and animals. There are fourteen bays with carvings featuring biblical stories from the Creation of Life, Noah's Ark, Samson and Delilah, the Tower of Babel and Rebecca at the Well to the Birth of Jesus, the Crucifixion, the Resurrection, the Ascension and, finally, the Day of Judgement.

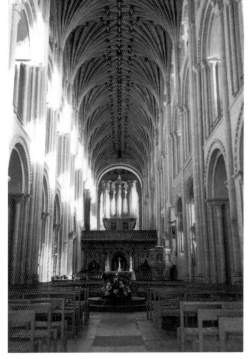

Above left: *The autumn sun captures the fine colour of the cathedral.*

Above right: *The second highest spire in the country.*

Left: *The high roof appears to be reaching to heaven.*

Opposite above: *Not much has changed since these early ground plans were drawn.*

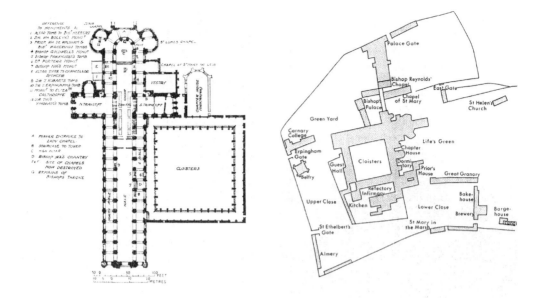

There is so much that is special about this cathedral. To start with, it has a Norman ground plan that has not been dramatically amended since its foundations were laid in 1091 by the determined character Bishop Herbert de Losinga, whose name means 'the flatterer'. It is said that he once bribed William II to make him Bishop of Thetford, and there are pictures in the cathedral depicting this. Before he died in 1119, he was able to see most of the magnificent structure completed and it remains virtually a monument to him. There is no doubt that without his drive and strength of character, coupled with his statesmanlike qualities, the cathedral would not have been built in such a short space of time. Unfortunately his tomb was destroyed by the Puritans during the Civil War but there is a slab that has a fine testimony inscribed by Dean Prideaux in the eighteenth century:

> *A MAN IMBUED WITH EVERY*
> *SORT OF LEARNING*
> *OF INCOMPARABLE ELOQUENCE*
> *HANDSOME IN PERSON*
> *AND OF BRIGHT COUNTENANCE*
> *SO THAT THESE, WHO KNEW HIM NOT*
> *MIGHT GUESS HE WAS A BISHOP*
> *ONLY FROM LOOKING AT HIM.*

Ravaged by fire on a number of occasions, damaged by citizens and Puritans, desecrated by Parliamentarian troops, it is a wonder that anything is left in the interior. Graffiti carved by musketeers can still be seen in the bays, and there is a stray musket ball still visible in Bishop

Bishop Goldwell's canopied tomb and the musket ball still embedded below his effigy.

Goldwell's tomb. At one time, the Puritans wanted the cathedral demolished so that the stones could be used to build a bridge at Great Yarmouth.

On one occasion, after yet another quarrel with the Benedictine monks, the citizens tried to burn the cathedral down. The damage was repaired quite quickly and the cathedral reconsecrated on Advent Sunday in 1278. The ceremony was carried out in the presence of Edward I and his Queen.

The addition of the Chancel House was completed in the year of Bishop Salmon in 1316. One of the four priests he endowed had the unenviable job of 'custos', which meant that he had to sing solo for his own soul, plus those of his parents, all his predecessors and successors in the see forever.

A spire was added to the tower in 1285 but it was blown down by a hurricane in 1361, creating much damage to the choir. Bishop Percy gave £400 out of his own purse to help towards the cost of repairs, during which a clerestory was added. Bishop Goldwell will always be remembered for building the spire in 1480. A thirteen-year-old boy sailor from Great Yarmouth once convinced the bishop's office to let him climb the spire to win a bet. He was given permission to look out of the upper window but, not content with that, the boy climbed out of the window, went to the top of the spire and pranced around it, spinning the weathercock at the same time. He returned quite safe and was not punished. In 1601, the spire was damaged by lightning but was quickly repaired.

Bishop Hall described in 1644 how the government troops were 'drinking and tobaconning' in the cathedral. They smashed windows, demolished monuments and stonework and destroyed the organ. Seats, vestments, hymnbooks and service books were taken outside and burnt in the marketplace. Perhaps the greatest treasure that survived is a painting on wood in the south aisle of the ambulatory. Originally a reredos in the Jesus Chapel, this rare work of outstanding beauty would certainly have been part of the bonfire in the marketplace if it had not been taken down and hidden by some unknown person, who carefully camouflaged it by turning it upside down, fitting four legs and using it as a table. It was discovered in the middle of the nineteenth century by Professor Willis. The painting bears the arms of Henry Spencer, the Fighting Bishop, who was alive in Chaucer's time. One of Spencer's relatives owned the Wilton Diptych, now in the National Gallery, which was painted by Thomas de Okell and it is thought that because of this connection, it was de Okell who did this painting too. The five panels contain extremely lifelike expressions on the faces of our Lord, the Madonna and the ruffians who are scourging Christ.

The ambulatory is full of other treasures, including a parchment by Losinga and another by Hugh Bigod. There is a fourteenth-century Domesday Book of the diocese and the Great Bible, bound in red morocco, on which Queen Victoria signed her Coronation Oath. A nice feature of the interior is the two little Jacobean men in white striped trousers, who are in the act of striking a bell with swords. These relics once formed part of an old clock and are situated under a modern clock in the south transept. There is also a collection, believed to be the finest in the

These Jacobean men are relics of an old clock.

world, of 1,500 of the rolls of the obedientiars, the twelve departmental executives responsible to the prior. The rolls are from 1ft to 10ft in length and if placed end to end would stretch over a mile and a half.

Considered by many to be of the finest quality stone and craftmanship in the cathedral, the fifteenth-century tomb of Bishop Goldwell contains nearly 100 arches and windows and has a smooth tracery of diamond and ring patterns. The bishop's life-size recumbent effigy shows him vested in a cope instead of the chasuble used in Mass or Holy Communion. This unequalled Gothic beauty is the only tomb of its kind to have survived the Reformation.

Nearby is another significant tomb, that of Sir William Boleyn, grandfather of Anne Boleyn. St Luke's chapel, built by Bishop Losinga, is on the south side and is unusual for being the parish church of St-Mary-in-the-Marsh. Oddly round in shape, its use was granted to the parishioners when their church was destroyed in the reign of Queen Elizabeth I. Its original fine Seven Sacrament font was retained. The Bishop's Throne stands in the middle arch of the apse, the same position as that in the Basilica or Roman Imperial law courts. Behind the throne is a backcloth embroidered in gold thread and worked by Queen Mary.

There are sixty-two perfectly carved monastic stalls, with misericords and canopies above. These are surely the most exquisite fifth-century work of their kind. The subjects of the carvings include a chorus line of ladies, as well as dogs, eagles, pelicans and human faces. There are birds, faces, miniature gargoyles and a crowned king on the armrests. Many tourists never spot this wonderful craftsmanship. The misereres include such diverse subjects as a squirrel eating nuts, a man on a pig, a monkey on a dog's back, monks, dragons, a mermaid, a knight in armour and a man forcing open a lion's mouth. The craftsmen must have had a sense of humour and, of course,

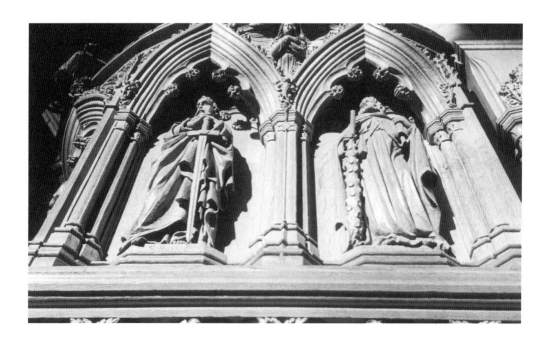

Above: An entertaining portrayal of life in the fifteenth century. One of many wonderful carvings in the misericords.

Opposite below: Two examples of fine woodcarving on a pulpit.

the fact that the bishops allowed them to do this work gives us an entertaining glimpse of life in those times. Mention must be made of one particular carving, which depicts an old lady with a spindle and distaff chasing after a fox who is galloping away with her chicken. While the lady is distracted, a pig is feasting quickly from her three-legged cooking-pot. There is also another carving of a monk feeding schoolboys with bread. Last but not least, there is an enchanting view of a shepherd tending his flock. All this adds up to scenes of beauty and oddities carved in the time of the Battle of Agincourt.

The cathedral has the largest monastic cloister in England. It has walks which are nearly 12ft wide surrounding a square of almost 170ft. The east walk was completed at the beginning of the fourteenth century and the cloister was finished when the north walk was completed around thirty years later. Changes in the design of the window tracery can be seen over this period. The vaulted stone roof has around 400 stone bosses and there is an upper storey – it is the only cloister with two storeys in England – where various records are kept in a library that includes many rare manuscripts and books, such as the Berners Book which was printed on Caxton's own press by his foreman, Wynkyn de Worde (an appropriate name for a printer!).

Among all the elaborate tombs and monuments, one important grave has been placed outside the building in a peaceful green corner. It has a small cross marking the resting place of nurse Edith Cavell, that wonderful martyr of the First World War. As a result of helping the British

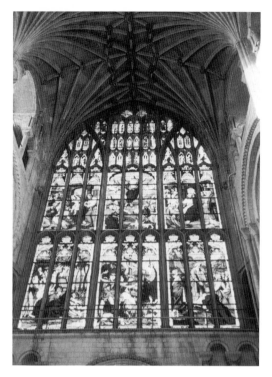 

Above left: *The beautiful stained-glass east window.*

Above right: *The simple but important grave of First World War martyr, nurse Edith Cavell.*

troops, she was shot by a German firing squad. Before the bullets hit her, she cried out the words that are inscribed on her grave:

Standing as I do, in view of God and Eternity, I realise that patriotism is not enough; I must have no hatred or bitterness toward anyone.

This saintly lady is one of the finest examples of the very spirit of Christianity.

In 1778, there was an incident in gardens near to Cathedral Close. Six suspicious-looking men were confronted by excise officers who had rightly suspected that they were smugglers. They had in their possession a half-anker of Geneva gin. It is not recorded whether this was to be delivered to someone within the cathedral. The officers seized the gin and were immediately attacked by the men. Seeing a fellow officer receiving a violent blow on the head, another drew his hanger and severely injured the assailant. The injured man was conveyed to the local hospital in a Hackney coach that was commandeered by the officers when it happened to pass by.

At the end of Cathedral Close is the old watergate, known to most people as Pull's Ferry. This very pretty and quiet corner is where the priors disembarked from their barges.

Pull's Ferry with the cathedral in the background.

Cattle Market Street

Running from Rose Lane to Golden Ball Street, this street was once known as Common Pump Street, as there was a pump at the junction with Golden Ball Street. In the sixteenth century, it was known as Beaumont's Hill or Buff Coat Lane because there was an inn called The Buff Coat near the entrance to Rouen Road, whose landlord was 'Father' Beaumont.

After the ditches were flattened on the south side of the castle, it was decided to hold a livestock market here every Saturday. Huge flocks of sheep were brought in for the market and the aptly named Woolpack public house was built, which was a favourite haunt for farmers and shepherds who came for a pint and a mardle. The market continued in one form or another right up until the 1960s when it was relocated to Hall Street, Harford in order to clear a space to create a parking area for the Castle Mall development.

In 1963, a large number of buildings were demolished to provide room for an approach road to Rouen Road, which had been constructed to relieve King Street. A year before this, a popular pub named the Golden Ball was demolished. Its sign, comprising a large golden ball, was retained and is now on display in Strangers' Hall.

Norwich foundries and engineering companies made wire netting, fire grates, manhole covers and many of the iron gates used on stately homes and big estates throughout the county. The beautiful nineteenth-century ironwork façade of one such firm, Holmes and Sons Ltd, can still be seen on a building in Cattle Market Street, opposite the southern entrance to the Castle Mall; it was based on a design taken from the Great Exhibition of 1851.

Regular sheep sales were held here every Saturday until the 1960s.

The unique nineteenth-century ironwork façade has been carefully maintained on this building in Cattle Market Street.

Chantry Road

Near to the theatre and the Assembly House, Chantry Road runs from Chapel Field East to Malthouse Road and was named after the chantry of the College of St Mary. One of the factories adjacent to this road was the Caley's chocolate factory, later owned by John Mackintosh. Norwich is proud to be associated with Albert Caley, who was born in Windsor on 29 October 1829. He was a chemist who opened a factory in this location because he found a deep well with the purest water in the city. Even in the 1880s, people would pay handsomely for bottles of the water. Caley's were originally known for high-quality ginger beer and medicated water but then Caley started to make a chocolate drink to supplement the water trade, especially in the winter when sales dropped. From there, he went on to manufacture chocolate.

Making chocolates by hand in the Caley's factory.

Caley expected his staff to follow his own example of working hard for six days a week, with no let-off for bank holidays, but he valued all his workers and, as a deeply religious man, he always took interest in his staff and their problems. It is thought that another reason for his move into the chocolate business was to ensure that his workers always had full employment. Ladies can be grateful to Caley's, for they hired a Frenchman whose skill sowed the seeds for the development of boxed chocolates, and he persuaded Albert to employ women in the factory. Even the famous artist Alfred Munnings worked on the designs for the sweet wrappers.

Lord Mackintosh, another influential and philanthropic man who was similar in many respects to Albert Caley, purchased Caley's in 1932. He once said: 'Caley's was the first chocolate I ever had as a child.' Mackintosh started his confectionery business during 1890 in Halifax, using his Granny Mack's simple recipe for toffee, which was based on a sack of sugar, salt and butter. There was also a recipe for macaroons and other pastries that were sold alongside the toffee. From this, the company grew into a worldwide industry and the products into household names. His heir was a true chip off the old block and lived an action-packed life. He still found time to be a family man as well as having a heavy involvement in public life. He was honoured with a knighthood at the age of thirty-one and was created a viscount in 1957.

Jno Mackintosh

Macaroon
1 lb granulated sugar
1/2 - ground almonds
mix with eggs

Toffee
4 lbs moist sugar
a small handfull of salt
two cupfull of water
12 oz butter
boil very quickly without the
butter, about 20 minutes, taking
of the skим, then drop in the
butter, and boil about 10
minutes, till it thickens, take
off before too brown.

Blanc Mange
1 quart of milk, 2 eggs, wisk, and
add, half an ounce of gelatine, add
the rind of a lemon, sugar to taste,
stir over a slow fire till thick, take out
the rind, and pour into the mould to set

ORIGINAL TOFFEE RECIPE
USED BY Mrs MACKINTOSH
✦ IN 1890. ✦
✖ ✦ ✖ ✦ ✖ ✦ ✖ ✦ ✖
WRITTEN JUST BEFORE HER
MARRIAGE, AND THE OPENING
OF THE SHOP IN KING CROSS LANE
✦   HALIFAX.   ✦

Above left: *Lord Mackintosh senior.*

Above right: *The first Mackintosh toffee was based on Granny Mack's recipe.*

Left: *A famous full-page newspaper advertisement for Mackintosh's toffee.*

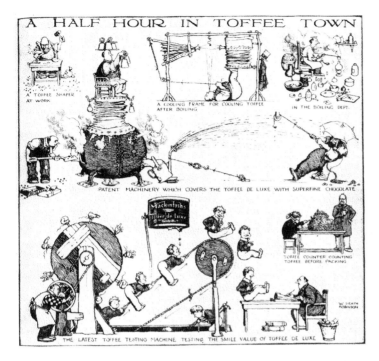

Left: *Heath Robinson's amusing cartoon depicting 'A Half Hour in Toffee Town'.*

Below left: *Mr Mackintosh's unusual landing in America.*

Below right: *A topical advertisement which appeared at the time of Shackleton's expedition to the South Pole.*

During the Second World War, troops received Caley's chocolate as part of their standard rations and it became a household name as the Marcho or marching chocolate bar. However, the factory was one of the many in the area that suffered badly in the so-called Baedeker raids of 1942. Norwich was one of the important places of historical interest in Britain that were detailed in the German *Baedeker's Guide* and was one of the cities highlighted as a target for bombing raids, which were reprisals for the murder of Heydrich, Himmler's deputy. The raids were responsible for over 60 per cent of the fatalities that occurred in the city during the whole of the Second World War.

During one of these raids – a thirty-bomber raid that lasted for two hours – the Caley's factory used their own water supply to try to quell the flames of an adjacent printing works that had suffered a direct hit, but unfortunately the water pressure was too low and the works burned down. Immediately afterwards, the chocolate factory itself received a direct hit from a high-explosive bomb. Six floors of the building were gutted and 1,000 tons of sweets went up in flames. The raid put paid to the Marcho chocolate bar and all types of Mackintosh products for the next fourteen years.

This particular bombing raid damage finished off most of the larger industries in the vicinity. Norwich burned all night with a red glow that could be seen miles from the city. However, most surprisingly, the principal ancient buildings of the city such as the cathedral, castle and guildhall remained intact, while properties surrounding them were flattened. This is reminiscent of the famous photograph of the dome of St Paul's Cathedral standing undamaged against the backdrop of a blitzed London.

The Duchess of Kent opened a new Mackintosh factory in 1956 but that was closed in the 1990s by Nestlé, who had acquired the business. The site is now part of a huge new shopping and housing development. Today, Caley's chocolate is being made once again, by a number of former managers who bought the brand in 1998. It is still regarded as a high-quality product, having been improved so that it is now much smoother and has a strong flavour which chocoholics love. It contains 70 per cent cocoa solids just like the original formula.

Chapel Field North – Chapel Field East – Chapel Field Road

These three roads form a triangle adjacent to part of the old city wall and enclose Chapelfield Gardens, an attractive park that used to have regular concerts in its bandstand. The park became a popular place for workers to rest during their lunchbreaks from the nearby chocolate factory of Rowntree Mackintosh.

On 14 July 1835, handbills were circulated in Norwich that announced 'the Dutch Hercules, Mynheer Kousewinkler van Raachboomstadt, professor of gymnastics and Maitre des Armes to the 5th Regiment of Royal Jaggers' would give his 'celebrated series of gymnastic exercises' in Chapel Field. Over 1,000 people crammed into the area to see this spectacle, only to find to their annoyance that it was all a hoax!

There used to be a fine Congregational chapel in this area, completed in the record time of fifteen months by Horace Sexton in 1858, at a cost of £3,500. At that time, Chapelfield was a

The bandstand or pavilion in the 1900s.

smart area in which to live. The chapel was demolished by the Norwich Corporation in 1972, as they were keen to expand the road system and develop the area.

In 1841, James Grigor of Old Lakenham Nursery published a fine illustrated work of remarkable trees, at a time when Norwich was called the City of Gardens. His concern was that the city had no botanical garden and he suggested that Chapelfield was the perfect spot because it had dignity and grace, coupled with good soil, plentiful supplies of water and some noble old trees.

In 2000, Morris dancers from the eastern region took part in a dancing marathon. They set off from the Royal Exchange in London on 15 April and arrived in Norwich on 22 April, beating Will Kemp's record by one day (*see* St John Maddermarket). They, however, did it in relays with no rest periods! Six dancers and two musicians completed the whole journey, including twenty-year-old Bethan McLachlan from Norwich who played her recorder the whole way. They danced in Chapelfield Gardens and then presented Lord Mayor Doug Underwood with a scroll before they went on to complete the dancing marathon. They even leapt over the wall at St John Maddermarket as Kemp did, and still had the energy to join in a party and ceilidh in St Andrew's Hall.

Charing Cross

The original name of Charing Cross was Tonsoria, a name derived from the Latin for 'premises where woollen cloth is cut'. The name later changed to Sherershil, which comes from 'shearing', referring to the trimming of the cloth. In the eighteenth century, the street was renamed Charing Cross after its namesake in London that was also home to a large number of textile workers.

The interior of Strangers' Hall.

On the left is Strangers' Hall, a merchant's house dating back to the fourteenth century. The name refers to the Protestant weavers who came to Norwich from the Netherlands in the sixteenth century. They brought new skills and techniques that transformed the Norfolk worsted industry, which was in the doldrums at that time. However, their arrival upset a few locals who nicknamed them 'strangers' and, as around thirty Dutch families stayed at this house, it became known as Strangers' Hall.

The house has a fifteenth-century hall with a fine crown roof. Nicholas Sotherton, who was mayor of Norwich in 1534, made additions to the house and it is a good example of a rich merchant's house with fine panelling, an old staircase, and a musicians' gallery. The rooms are furnished with care and all the effects indicate what life would have been like for wealthy people in past centuries. There are collections of domestic utensils, clothes, tools, firearms and personal bits and pieces. In addition, there are lazy-tongs, velocipedes, whips, spurs, fowling-pieces, spinets, cradles, watchmen's rattles and even mantraps, which were used to catch unsuspecting intruders. The house still has the lived-in feeling which is so often lost in larger stately homes. Strangers' Hall was turned into a museum by Leonard Bolingbroke, a local solicitor and grandson of Norwich School artist James Stark, and presented to the city in 1922.

Church Alley

Several houses of note are to be found in this alley, which is just off Colegate. There is a fine fifteenth-century flint-built house that was once owned by a Quaker wine merchant named Sparswell, whose son was an artist of some repute and a student of John Crome. Another flint house, which was the town house of the Prior of Ixworth, can also be seen and, next to that, a rich merchant's house dating from the eighteenth century.

Colegate

Duke Street divides this road into two parts. Its name probably comes from the family name Cole, which is a name much in evidence in the county. For example, Henry Cole of Wroxham, Walter Cole of St Faith's and Richard Cole of Wymondham. All these families go back as far as the twelfth century.

Together with the nearby area of St Georges, Colegate was the home of many rich and successful merchant classes. They were mainly Nonconformists, hence the number of Nonconformist chapels here. Several of the three-storey houses were inhabited by journeyman shoemakers, who worked in the attics. The area later became the location of several boot and shoe factories, including one owned by Norvic Shoes. This was one of the largest in Britain and the company were the biggest employer in Norwich for many years. Their manufacturing processes were similar to the mass production system of car factories. The factory closed in 1980 and has been converted into flats, shops, offices and restaurants.

Opposite Calvert Street is the Merchants public house, which was previously called The Blackboys. The old name is preserved in Blackboys Yard to the rear, where there was once a School for Young Gentlewomen run by Sarah Glover and her sisters.

Between Calvert Street and St Georges a restored group of houses with lucam gables can be seen. There is also Bacon House, a large fifteenth-century timber-framed house, now converted into flats. It was once the home of Henry Bacon, a wealthy worsted merchant who was sheriff and twice mayor of Norwich, in 1557 and 1566. During his first term of office as mayor, he became very upset when a weaver's wife was burnt to death because of her Protestant faith. He was cheered in his second term of office, for he was able to welcome Protestant Dutch weavers to the city. The weavers were responsible for reviving the dying cloth trade in the region.

The home of Henry Bacon, a wealthy and influential man in fifteenth-century Norwich.

In St George's church is the grave of painter Old John Crome. He died in 1821 at the early age of fifty-three and there is a fine memorial plaque on a wall inside the church.

The Octagon Chapel was designed and built by Thomas Ivory in 1756. Wesley thought the Octagon chapel was the most elegant chapel in Europe; others who were less charitable called it 'the devil's cucumber frame'. It has a fine wrought-iron finial and ball provided in 1975 with the help of donations from the Anglia Square and Magdalen Street Traders' Association. The chapel occupies the site of the medieval church of St John the Baptist, used by the Black Friars from 1226 until early 1307, when they moved to St Andrews Hall. The friars, whose name comes from the colour of their robes, became popular and influential because they lived a spartan life and went out among the people speaking in a basic language that everyone easily understood.

Coslany Street

At one time, a huge number of working families lived in squalid conditions in alleys off this street. In St John's Head Yard, a family of forty-six were found housed in one building. There were several properties which had rooms below ground level; these basement rooms were called 'dybtes' or 'holes' and were often subject to flooding from the drains of nearby streets. Typhoid fever was a common killer amongst the inhabitants. It must be remembered that there was no refuse collection in those days: waste and muck was left to accumulate in the streets together with excrement from pigsties. It wasn't until the end of the nineteenth century, after the Public Health Act of 1872 came into force, that the Norwich water supply and sewerage systems were finally improved.

In 1752, a young lad who became a printer's apprentice was born in this parish. His name was Luke Hansard and he became the official printer of the debates in the House of Commons. He had an exceptional memory and a willingness to learn. He went to London with a guinea in his pocket and made a fortune from printing the reports of parliamentary proceedings. At that

The interior of the unusual Octagon chapel.

Once a mill producing various cloths, including worsted, this building later became a printing works.

time they were sold for 5p in today's money, but with sales volumes of over 6,000 this money went a long way towards securing his future. To this day the reports of the debates are called the *Hansard*.

Cotman Fields

During Kett's Rebellion in 1549, one of the most horrific deaths was that of Lord Sheffield. His horse failed in an attempt to jump a ditch near the Great Hospital and threw him virtually into the arms of the rebels. Hoping to become a hostage, he took his helmet off to identify himself but the rebels had no respect for nobility and he was bludgeoned to death. His head was cut off in one blow by a local butcher named Fulke.

Cowgate

The name of this street gives a good indication of its history. Cows were driven along here from pastures in nearby Cowholme. Originally it connected Magdalen Street to Whitefriars Bridge but is now split by the roundabout on the Inner Ring Road.

Norwich Yarn Company built a five-storey factory in Cowgate during 1834. It contained a steam-powered mill that was the first of its kind in Norwich. In the early nineteenth century, Norwich became the largest silk producing centre in England and was noted for designs made from both cheap and luxurious materials. The fashionable Norwich shawl was first made of cotton and worsted, then silk and worsted and, finally, one of pure silk was added to the range. These sold for between £10 and £15 and brought the wages of the silk weavers up to £10 a week. At the same time, powered machinery was spreading into other industries and this was to have a disturbing effect on all labour-intensive work, particularly agriculture.

At the start of the First World War, the factory became a chocolate factory. Later, Jarrold's the printers needed more premises so they bought it and converted it into a printing works.

Cow Hill

Although it was a major connecting road between Pottergate and Upper St Giles Street, Cow Hill did not appear on early maps of the city. The street took its name from an eighteenth-century pub called the Red Cow, which was situated next door to St Giles parish hall in a side road called Cow Yard.

Cross Lane

This small lane is named after the medieval Cow Cross that once stood at its junction with Calvert Street and was where the city cowherd gathered in the citizens' cows. On its north side is the Little Portion Mission House, a mission associated with the Sisters of All Hallows, Ditchingham. The building used to be the Rifleman Alehouse, where the Dirty Shirt Club – a group of weavers in their scruffy workwear – met here after work on Saturday afternoons. They received their wages from the master weaver, who was paid back in free drinks.

The alehouse was a favourite haunt of artist John Crome. He was used to alehouses, having been born in the Griffin public house in Tombland, where his father was the landlord. John was quite bright but had little education. He developed an impish sense of humour and was fond of playing jokes on people. When he worked at Dr Rigby's surgery in St Giles, he changed the labels on patients' medicine bottles and was finally fired for throwing a skeleton out of an upstairs window at some students. He was apprenticed to a signwriter and became a famous and wealthy artist. His style developed into what is known as the Norwich School and his landscapes sold for huge amounts. In spite of this, his feet remained firmly on the ground and he returned to the Rifleman Alehouse to meet his friends on so many occasions that he had his own chair.

D

Davey Place

This street is named after Alderman Jonathan Davey (1760-1814), who lived the high life in Eaton Hall where he gave some grand parties. He is remembered for many incidents, including once when his house was put under police guard for twenty-four hours a day after he was overheard to say he wanted to put a hole in the King's head. The police were suspicious because Davey, an astute businessman who became a director of Norwich Union, had a reputation as a Baptist and an extreme radical and had many friends who were in favour of the French Revolution. However, what he really meant was that he wanted to put a hole in the King's Head pub that he had purchased, to provide easy access from the Market Place direct to the Castle Ditches. The steps bearing his name became the first traffic-free road in Norwich, opened for pedestrians only in 1813. Davey Place continues to this day to be a useful shortcut.

The King's Head became a very busy Georgian coaching inn where the famous Parson Woodforde, a Norfolk clergyman and eighteenth-century diarist, stayed. The inn had a very busy night in 1767 when crowds flocked in to see the massive Irish giant O'Brien. He was 8ft 4in tall and his head nearly touched the ceilng.

Mr J.M. Murray lived in Davey Place. He was the 'sole agent for the sale of Bridgman's patent iron coffins for the security to the deceased persons'. A lot of bodysnatching went on at this time to provide surgeons with bodies for dissection and Murray saw an opportunity to allay the fears of families who had lost loved ones.

Dove Street

Before the seventeenth century, landlord John Riches made the Dove Inn so popular that it gave its name to the street. Dove Street was known as Holdtor – meaning 'ditch tower', a predecessor of the tollhouse, later to become the guildhall – Lane because a small river ran through it to a tower at one end.

Duke Street

Originally only a small street, it was extended in the 1800s and now runs from the Inner Ring Road at St Crispin's right into the centre of the city. The palace of the Dukes of Norfolk on the south bank of the river, close to the bridge, was built in around 1602 but most of it was demolished a century later in 1711.

E

Elm Hill

In the reign of Henry VIII, there was a triangular piece of open land at the top of this street with two huge elm trees. Sadly, these succumbed to disease and were replaced by a plane tree. This narrow cobbled street, which slopes up to its junction with Princes Street, contains the oldest inn in Norwich, the Britons' Arms, which was built in Elizabethan times and has a thatched roof. Every new visitor to Norwich comes to Elm Hill to look at the attractive small properties, which have long been a popular subject for artists and are frequently photographed for calendars and prints. It is hard to believe that this was once a very squalid street, having a mixture of medieval and Victorian houses of no real significance.

In the thirteenth century, the Friars de Sacco, who dressed in penitential sackcloth, had their base here. The Black Friars were granted a licence to take over the order when their numbers dwindled and they eventually moved to the new church at St Andrews.

Above left: Autumn leaves starting to fall from the plane tree in Elm Hill. Above right: On the right is the Britons' Arms, which has retained its Elizabethan qualities.

In the fifteenth century, Elm Hill became a very fashionable place and the wealthy Paston family had a house here, built by Augustine Steward. As great benefactors to the city, the family are also well known for founding the Paston Grammar School in North Walsham, where Lord Nelson was a pupil. John Pettus, a friend of the Pastons who was mayor in 1590, lived nearby. Many of his descendants have moved to the United States but they still make pilgrimages to Elm Hill and their family church, St Simon and St Jude's, has survived demolition largely due to their financial help.

At the top of Elm Hill is a museum of church art in what was St Peter Hungate church. It houses a good collection of church plate, a silver cross decorated with a ball of Blue John stone and amethysts. There are musical instruments, including a hand organ that was typically used in village churches, and beautifully illustrated books from the fourteenth century.

The street has a number of fine antique shops and the Strangers' Club, which at one time claimed to be a place where 'you can eat meat sliced from a whole calf cooked on a huge fire that could burn half a tree'. The club burned down in 1507, killing a family, and in the building that replaced it footsteps are often heard, even when there's nobody in.

The properties in Elm Hill date from the fourteenth or fifteenth century and there are a number of attractive alleys and courtyards to be seen. Thanks must go to the Norwich Society, who saved the Elm Hill area and its delightful properties from demolition. Unfortunately they could not influence the boring design of City Hall, which is in stark contrast to this charming location.

Above left: *The Masonic tavern was a popular haunt for members of the 'craft'.*

Above right: *One of the many courts and alleys leading off Elm Hill.*

Left: *The Strangers' Club building, famous for its large fireplace and its resident ghost.*

Exchange Street

Once known as Old Post Office Street, this was the first new road built in the city since the Norman period. It has also been called Museum Street, after the Norfolk and Norwich Museum built on the site of the Duke of Norfolk's palace at St Andrews Street. The street takes its current name from the elegant Corn Exchange, built in 1828 at a cost of £6,000. 'Agricultural Gentlemen of Norfolk' subscribed £2,000 towards the total. It was replaced in 1863 by a more attractive building that lasted until demolition in 1964. The present Corn Exchange building is on the site of

Sir Benjamin's Court, where the first paintings ever displayed by the Norwich School of Art were exhibited in 1805. All but a few paintings were sold very quickly and from then on it became an annual event. Norwich became the first city outside London to hold such an annual exhibition.

On 13 December 1886, a crime occurred here that would go down in Norfolk's history. Within a few hours of being released from the city jail after serving a sentence for assaulting his wife, George Harmer made up an excuse to call on an old carpenter named Henry Last. He beat Last to death with a hammer and stole whatever money and possessions he could carry away. He covered the old man with sacks and went straight to London. Being somewhat of a recluse, the poor old man was not discovered for several hours but Harmer was under arrest within four days because the police had traced him through his luggage that had been forwarded on to him. Harmer confessed to his crime, which was out of character for him, and he became the last man to be hanged at Norwich Castle.

More recently, another crime was committed in a café here. Three local men visited the café in the early hours of the morning to pour petrol through the letterbox. Two of the men walked away but the third man, who ignited the petrol, was injured in the resultant explosion. He became the only known man to cross Exchange Street without touching the ground and was thrown against the solid wall of the Corn Hall on the opposite side of the road. The affair caused great activity in the local CID and led to a long period of police hospital duty while the culprit recovered. The explosion closed Exchange Street for some time and completely destroyed the café.

F

Farmers Avenue

This street was named after the Jolly Farmers Inn, and skirted the south side of the Old cattle market.

Fishergate

Herring and other fish were in plentiful supply in medieval times and there was a concentration of fisherman living in this parish of St Edmunds on the banks of the River Wensum. They landed their catches on St Edmund's Quay.

In his will, Thomas Anguish, who was mayor in 1611, endowed a children's hospital that was built in Fishergate principally for the very young and poor children of the city. Here they learned to read and write and then the boys were trained as craftsmen and the girls were taught the basics of housecraft. The children were called 'bluecoats' or 'bluebottles' because of their very smart uniforms: the boys wore tailed coats, striped waistcoats and red caps and the girls had blue gowns, scarves and poke bonnets. The school was closed in 1855, when it was decided to put more boys into secondary education and apprenticeships. The girls had been transferred in the seventeenth century to a school in Golden Dog Lane, which was created by an endowment from Robert Baron, who was mayor in 1649. A blind alley called Thoroughfare Yard connects Fishergate to Magdalen Street.

Friars Quay

The history of this quay goes back to the fourteenth century when it was owned by the Black Friars and used to transport goods from the river to their warehouses. The city council acquired the land and in the 1970s it became the first reclaimed riverside site in the city to become a housing project.

Fye Bridge Street

The name is based on its thirteenth century name Fibridgestrete, and then Fybrydggate Strete in the fifteenth century. This is probably the shortest stretch of road in Norwich. It spans the river, connecting Magdalen Street to Wensum Street. The only remaining building dating from before the nineteenth century is the tower of St Clement's church.

A Tudor ducking, or 'cucking', stool was sited here and provided great entertainment for the Norwich population. Processed in by people beating drums and cymbals and blowing horns, the unfortunate woman – who had been accused of being a prostitute, a witch or a strumpet – would be brought in by cart and dunked in the cold, dirty river. How many times depended on her crime.

In the early part of the nineteenth century, trams came to Norwich. Electric Tramway No. 1 terminated at Fye Bridge after its journey from St Catherine's Plain.

The 1930s bridge is the fifth on this site and was erected to provide work for the unemployed. However, this was a strange decision because the construction of the bridge caused the loss of jobs, as a large number of family-owned businesses had to be demolished so that the road could be widened to take the increased volume of traffic.

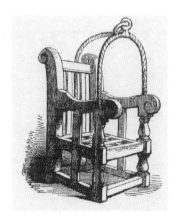

The ducking stool was attached to a long pole over the foulest water at Fye Bridge.

G

Gentleman's Walk

There were many occasions when the gentlemen of the county came to the city; they often came to meet visiting royalty and dignitaries or to attend the courts or sessions. This street was their usual place to walk together, dressed in fine long coats with silver buttons and buckled shoes, and carrying silver-topped canes. Here they would digest considerable amounts of information and even larger lunches.

Known as the Walk, it is now virtually closed to all traffic and it is hard to imagine that in the early nineteenth century it was full of horse-drawn vehicles and trams that used two sets of lines. The noise from these echoed from the shop buildings, many of which have retained their original façades. The trams were almost as colourful as the striped canopies of the nearby market stalls, as each tram destination board had a different colour to identify its route. Newmarket Road was green, Unthank Road black and white, Eariham Road had a red border and some even had two colours if the routes overlapped. Passengers found this easier to remember than numbers.

In 1788, the city celebrated the centenary of the Glorious Revolution. There was extra excitement when a huge tiger, part of a travelling menagerie brought for display at the Bear Inn in the Walk, broke loose and could not be secured until he had eaten two monkeys, horrifying

This fine nineteenth-century print from an engraving shows part of Gentleman's Walk and the market place, with Norwich Castle in the background.

the assembled crowd. The tiger did not survive long because the collar and chain he had eaten in order to escape 'gangreened within him and killed the beast'.

The original Royal Hotel was situated here and its façade is still visible as part of the entrance into the ornate arcade. Its operating licence was transferred to the large gothic building in Bank Plain.

Robert Hales, a celebrated Norfolk giant, used to sell the story of his life for a penny a time on Gentleman's Walk. He died on 22 November 1863, aged forty-three. At his peak, he stood 7ft 6in tall, measured over 5ft around his waist and weighed 33 stones. Queen Victoria received him in court and he met nobility across the world. In 1848, he went to America, where he joined Barnum and Bailey's Circus as the Tallest Man in the World. When he finally returned to Norfolk in 1851, he was without funds and reduced to selling his life story. Even his poor sister, who was over 6ft tall, appeared with him on tour. He died penniless in the Yarmouth workhouse and is buried in a large tomb in Somerton churchyard.

Gildencroft

Gentlemen belonging to various guilds met here and the name means 'guild brethren's croft'. In earlier times, this was an area where jousting – a word that comes from 'justing acre' – took place.

Golden Ball Street

The street takes its name from an old inn. It may at one time have been called Barningham Stile but scholars still disagree on this point. What is certain is that alterations to Castle Hill in 1862 transformed the area beyond recognition.

The Woolpack public house was situated opposite the cattle market and was very convenient for the farmers and buyers. An army recruitment drive took place near here. In the 1940s large Wolseley police cars came into full use, one such new and shiny car with two proud occupants escorted a low-loader lorry carrying a huge tank into Golden Ball Street. The tank was to be unloaded at a prearranged spot in a lane, from where it could be driven a short distance to an open area, to be admired by young men who might potentially throw in their lot for the army. The Wolseley drove to the end of the lane and turned around to watch the unloading of the tank. The policemen could clearly see the tank churning uphill towards them but assumed that the tank driver could see the Wolseley and would stop to let it pass. However, the forty-ton tank kept going. The driver at the helm knew very little about driving tanks. 'Just move it up the lane he had been told, with no explanation of the techniques involved with hydraulic pressure in relation to braking efficiency. The eyes looking through the aperture were stricken with panic as the driver fumbled with the controls. The policemen had no time to find reverse gear in the Wolseley and had to jump out of the car as the tank climbed over the bonnet and stopped at the windscreen. The Wolseley was scrap and the red-faced policemen spent days writing their report.

The unfortunate police car.

Golden Dog Lane

This ancient lane dates back to the twelfth century, when it was called the Common Lane. It was at one time called Brent Lane after the church of St Mary the Burnt or 'brent', a name that dates from the time of the Conquest when there was a great fire in the area that demolished the church's thatched roof. The church was torn down after the Dissolution. The lane takes its current name from the Golden Dog alehouse that existed for a short period in 1626 and was replaced by another inn of the same name, which closed after the great flood of 1912.

Grapes Hill

This follows the route of the old city wall and there are remains of the wall to be seen at the northern end. There is not much of the hill left because it was levelled to make room for the Inner Link Road. Originally there was a pub here called The Grapes, which marked the boundary of the parish of Heigham. It once had a lead boundary mark showing the unfortunate St Ethelbert being flayed.

Guildhall Hill

Work started on the guildhall in 1407, just three years after the city received its charter. It was built using stone and flint in fine patterns. Residents of Norwich were press-ganged, on the threat of being arrested, to work for upwards of fifteen hours a day on the guildhall. Perhaps the use of this forced unskilled labour was the reason why the towers fell down in 1508, although it is more likely a result of collapsing tunnels from the old chalk and saltpetre mines underneath the city. The roof followed suit three years later and 123 years afterwards, the whole hall started to shift.

Judges, Sheriffs and civic leaders made their decisions in the guildhall for 500 years. Guilds, trades and their appropriate apprenticeships were approved here. The city robes and insignia, records and tax collection all had space in the building. Citizens who could not write were able to pay scribes to produce letters or legal documents and this took place privately in soundproofed booths.

The city gaol was conveniently situated at the end of the building. Ordinary prisoners were housed on the ground floor; the most violent were held in the undercroft dungeons. If a prisoner wanted to repent of his sins, this could be done in a small chapel that had a spiral staircase directly connected to the dungeons. In 1597, the prison was relocated to the former inn known as the Lamb. In 1826, it moved to the large City Gaol and House of Correction that had been built at St Giles Gate at a cost of £30,000. In 1884, this site was totally cleared to make room for the Roman Catholic cathedral that was completed in 1910.

This picture of the 1920s guildhall was taken before City Hall was built.

The guildhall clock tower is Victorian, as is much of the outside decoration on the building. The guildhall was one of many important buildings in the city which were heavily sandbagged during the Second World War. Panic hit the city on the first day of the war when the air-raid siren was sounded but it turned out to be a false alarm and Norwich had a clear run for over ten months until the first damaging raid occurred on 9 July 1940. By the time the war was over, nearly 1,500 alerts had been sounded and on a number of occasions bombs were dropped, often by a single aircraft, before any warnings were given. It took a meeting of the city council with the Ministers of Home Security in London to sort the warning system out.

The guildhall is now a tourist attraction. It has a restaurant that features some Caley's products, especially chocolate which was originally manufactured in Norwich and became known as the Armies Marching Chocolate during both World Wars (*see* Chantry Road). The historic layout of the courtroom has been retained with galleries and enclosures, creating a unique atmosphere.

On special occasions or ceremonials, the Lord Mayor travels in the city coach, drawn by horses provided by a local brewery. On one such day, he was accompanied by the High Court judge, both of them dressed in splendid robes. The coach was steered by ornately dressed brewery drivers, who did their best to prevent the procession from hesitating outside public houses with the relevant brewery allegiance, as the horses were used to stopping for deliveries. Unfortunately, someone forgot to sand the steep Guildhall Hill and the poor horses were stepping and sliding on the spot, much to the annoyance of their illustrious passengers who found themselves with the same view for some time.

H

Hansard Lane

This street perpetuates the name of Luke Hansard (*see* Colegate). Born into a poor family in the eighteenth century, he went on to make a fortune and when he died he left over £80,000 in his will.

Nearby is the oldest round tower church in Norwich: St Edmund's. Its churchyard is thought to be the place where Saxon drovers rested their cattle overnight, on their way to the city market.

The lane was flooded during the great flood of 1912, when the whole of Norwich was cut off from the rest of the world. Three people were killed in the city and four children in Hansard Lane had to be saved by Norwich police when their panic-stricken parents couldn't reach them.

Hay Hill

Just off Haymarket, this street has a name which is a reminder of the trade that was once carried out here. This type of business and other rural trades were relocated in the late eighteenth century to the ditches around the castle.

Hay Hill has attracted a lot of controversy, especially when C&A built their modern square-shaped store (now Next) here in 1970. The store occupies the site of Alderman Riseborough's School for Poor Boys, which later became a brush factory and then a warehouse. Outside the store is a statue of Sir Thomas Browne (*see* Haymarket).

Today, this open area is being put to good use, especially when the French Market comes to Norwich, selling croissants, freshly baked bread and cheese that can be washed down with Bordeaux. On one memorable occasion there was a lady accordion player serenading the casual diners. On addressing her in his schoolboy French, the author was surprised to find that she was not French but a member of staff in City Hall, as well as being a first-class musician and a member of the city's Accordion Band. The French Market is not warmly received by all the city's market stallholders, some of whom feel that they lose trade.

Two ancient inns are visible here: the White Hart and the Cambridge, which in 1860 was the Barley Mow.

Haymarket

The White Swan in Haymarket was a busy coaching inn, although some of its guests were not always what they seemed. In 1779, smuggling was rife throughout the country and Norwich citizens, fed-up with the number of smugglers operating in the city, took matters into their own hands. Revenue forces were not well organised and, looking at the service as a whole, the quality of the men recruited may in part have made the force less effective. In one period of seven years, between 1821 and 1827, 229 men were dismissed for drunkenness, outrageous conduct, insubordination or connection with smugglers. On dismissal, some actually joined the smugglers. When the Lynn coach arrived at the White Swan inn one day in July, on board were a naval lieutenant and his press gang, who were to stand trial for impressing the servants of an important Lynn merchant. Rumour had spread throughout the city that they were smugglers armed with pistols. A crowd got together and arrested them, and they were jailed for several hours before the lieutenant arrived with the subpoenas and they were released.

Extensive changes occurred to these streets, largely due to the disappearance of the trams and war damage. The popular grocer's, County and City Supplies was owned by a well-known personality in Norwich, Edward Wild. He was an alderman of the city, a director of Norwich Union and later received a knighthood. Another grocer, Gerald Dodson, had similar premises to Wild, which were also taken over by International Stores. Dodson received a knighthood as well. Famous medical man, Sir Thomas Browne, lived at No. 1 Haymarket. The author of *Religio Medici*, Browne was a philosopher and meticulous naturalist and knew a great deal about medieval folklore. There is a statue of him in Hay Hill.

Horns Lane

This lane was at one time connected to King Street. It takes its name from a pair of buck's horns found in Conesford Street. During the demolition of King Street in 1950, the builders found a Bellarmine jar (a stoneware jar decorated with a bearded face) at the point where King Street used to meet Horns Lane. It is thought to date from the seventeenth century and contained human fingernails, different coloured human hair and a quantity of iron nails. Local opinion is that it was used in ceremonies of witchcraft.

K

Ketts Hill

A small area near the roundabout on this part of the Inner Ring Road, Ketts Hill was once known as Spitalfields. It contains Victorian houses, a bakery and a pub and became the first built-up area on this side of the river.

King Street

This long and ancient road is steeped in history. It goes back to Saxon times when they first settled along the river and was probably one of the first roads in Norwich. The southern end of King Street was once called Southgate, as it was close to the now mostly demolished church of St Peter Southgate. There were churches, pubs and factories mixed in with houses owned by rich Jews and wealthy families like the Howards, before they became Dukes of Norfolk. Lady Catherine Howard, the niece of the third Duke of Norfolk, was Henry VIII's fifth wife and Henry Howard, the sixth Duke, built himself a house in King Street before he got the title. At the rear of the house, there was a wilderness area, bowling green and a cultivated garden. This area was known as a gentleman's country retreat and long after the Duke's death it was still referred to as 'My Lord's Garden'. The Duke was given the office of Earl Marshal of England, a rank held by all his successors.

In 1510, John Caius was born in the parish of St Etheldred, whose church in King Street had a traditional round tower. He initially wanted to become a clergyman but turned to medicine, studying and graduating in Padua. Most famous for his published work on the plague that killed nearly 1,000 people in the city, he became very wealthy and was at one time physician to Edward VI. He refounded his old college, Gonville, at Cambridge and it still bears his name. To this day, dining privileges there are still extended to senior members of the University of East Anglia.

Morgan's was a famous local brewery located in King Street. The street runs parallel to the River Wensum, from which boats landed the brewery's malt, barley and grain. One very sad day, director Walter Morgan, one of the founders, was inspecting a vat of fermenting beer. He was overcome by its fumes of carbonic acid, toppled into the vat and was drowned in his own beer.

In 1939, the government held an inquiry, under the Housing Act, to look at proposals to improve the street. This met with considerable opposition from the general public.
Experts from London were called in to give their view, which was to retain what they considered were the best examples of Dutch influence in the county. Many properties had large high weavers' windows that illuminated the attic floor. Among the buildings forming the Read Woodrow mills was the Albion Mill, which started off producing worsted yarn and then silk. By the end of the nineteenth century, it was a confectionery factory. In spite of the expert opinion, the city council ignored all advice and they got their way: the Minister concurred with them that everything had to be demolished.

At a narrow part of this street, close to Rose Lane, there used to be a butcher's shop owned by a Mr Wiseman. He had a pony and cart that would frequently block the path of electric trams. It was not long before the pony learned to move across the road to let the tram through and then return back to the shop unassisted.

The Waterman Arms at No. 142 King Street was rebuilt during the 1920s. The landlord was the local barber as well as publican. The pub had a famous sign bearing these words:

Roam not from Pole to Pole but step in here
Where nought excels the shaving, but the beer.

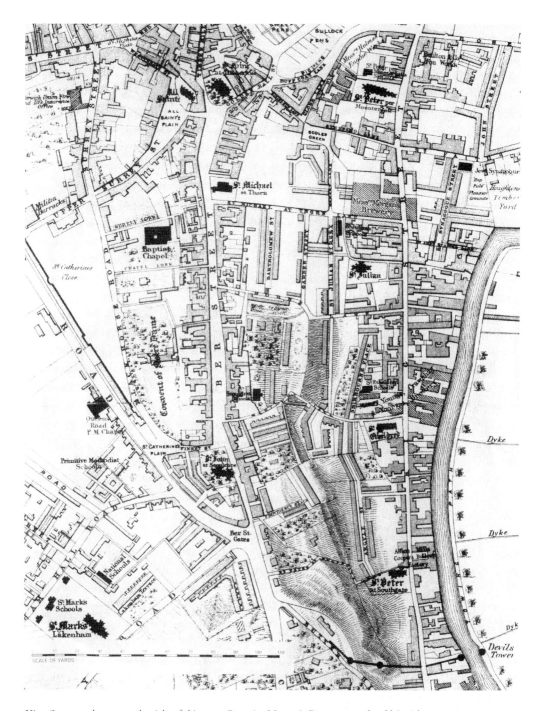

King Street can be seen to the right of this map. Opposite Morgan's Brewery was the old Jewish area.

A few yards outside the city wall, just past where King Street meets with Carrow Road, is the factory site of Colman's Mustard. This is one of the many industries that were affected by the Great Flood of 1912. All work stopped when rain created a huge landslide at Carrow Abbey, putting the electrical station under water and leaving everywhere in total darkness. The factory cellars, where starch was being stored, were under 3ft of water. The starch acted like a sponge and 650 tons of the expensive material was ruined. This sticky material was not easy to remove: the only way was to drill large holes in the floor and pass it up by hand through a chain of men. It must have been a strange sight because the men were naked and had to work by lamplight! Colman's were a prime target during the war and were hit several times, with many casualties and some deaths.

The Albion Mill was demolished, like many Dutch-influenced buildings in this street.

The Colman family and their employees, late nineteenth century.

The church of St Julian had a late Saxon tower but unfortunately the church was hit by a large bomb during the Second World War and this left only the north wall and porch standing. It was rebuilt using much of the original materials, supplemented by a Norman doorway from the nearby rubble of St-Michael-at-Thorn church. It was in St Julian's that the Lady Julian of Norwich lived the life of an anchoress for forty years, confined in a tiny cell attached to the church. Here she wrote the first book to be written in English by a woman, The Revelations of Divine Love, based on the visions she received on 8 May 1373. Although the cell was destroyed at the Reformation, a chapel was built on the site and attracts pilgrims and tourists from all over the world, who come to relax and pray in this holy place.

The character of this street has been lost for all time due to the building of Rouen Road, which has taken people and business away from the area. It has now become a major route in and out of the city for both cars and pedestrians.

L

Lollards Road

Almost opposite Bishops Bridge is a site of gruesome interest: Lollard's Pit, a hollow close to where St Leonard's Priory once stood. Morbid processions led by monks and priests took prisoners carrying their own bundles of sticks to the stake here, where they were burned to a terrible death in front of bloodthirsty crowds. Many martyrs were made, such as Thomas Bilney, who had preached against abuses in the Church, and Elizabeth Cooper, who, on recanting her

The terrible end of one unfortunate woman provided entertainment for the crowd at Lollard's Pit.

faith, tried to convince others not to follow her example. Cicely Orme went to the pit merely as an onlooker but took pity on two dying criminals and comforted them. She was later tried and sentenced to an identical death for her trouble.

London Street

The original name of this street was Hosiergate, from the hosiers – who were makers of stockings – who used to trade here. The street has been home to a multitude of other retailers, from goldsmiths to cutlers. Part of the street east of Swan Lane was first called London Lane, partly due to the vast number of shops and trades and the huge volume of carts, coaches and horses, which resembled London. It became Cutlers Row in the fourteenth century, from the people trading in cutlery and surgical instruments. One of the largest was John Grimes, who traded into the nineteenth century.

These buildings in London Street have changed very little since this picture was taken in the late 1960s, and it is still a shopping precinct.

Men at work, not on the street but portrayed on the frieze below the flower-bedecked balcony of Jarrold's department store.

Albert Jarmen Caley, destined to be a famous chocolatier moved into this street and opened a chemist's shop in 1857. This is where, six years later, he started to make mineral waters in a cellar. He tested the market and his product was an instant success, so he was forced to find bigger premises in the city.

Jarrold's department store is located on the eastern corner of London Street, where it meets Exchange Street. It was the first location of their printing works and is now a popular store, which is still a family-owned business. One of their family, Samuel Jarrold, was a fine preacher and missionary with his own religious following. He was held in such high esteem that, on his death, all public houses on the route of his funeral closed for the day as a mark of respect.

This street has a number of attractive properties, the most important being the office of George Skipper, a famous Norwich architect. He was a pupil of the Norwich School of Art, where he won many prizes for his 'freehand, geometry and model'. In this street, Jarrold's have retained an elaborate frieze on their modern building on which Skipper depicts men at work under his direction. Even his family is included, with the family pet dog. There is evidence of his favourite Baroque style on many other buildings in the city and also the county, principally his hotels in Cromer.

Garland's was another popular department store on the corner of this street, at the junction with Little London Street. It burned down in 1970 when a chip-pan fire in the restaurant kitchen caused a fire that raged for seven hours. The cost of repairing the damage was around £1 million and it was only the sterling efforts of the city firemen that prevented the fire from spreading throughout London Street.

Little London Street

This alley once formed a route from London Street to St Andrew's Street. Its earliest name was Hosyergate, but this usually referred to London Street. It was also called Smithy Lane because of the blacksmiths who concentrated their business here.

Magdalen Gate from the outside.

M

Magdalen Street

Originally extending to Tombland, this street took its name from the chapel and hospital of St Mary Magdalen outside the city wall. On the road to Sprowston, approximately where St Crispin's Road crosses this street, was Stumps Cross – meaning 'the broken cross' – an ancient landmark which was demolished in the late fifteenth century then re-erected 108 years later, only to be taken down after four years and placed in nearby St Saviours churchyard where it remained until the late nineteenth century. The area is still called Stumps Cross by some people in a derisive way.

Using government money and funds raised by the city, the street was improved and modernised in 1970. This venture proved very successful and was the forerunner of similar projects throughout the United Kingdom. At first, this area created a lot of pride in Norfolk, with a new Odeon cinema, shops, restaurants and high office blocks that included Her Majesty's Stationery Office, but with the expansion of the city that is still taking place this area is probably no longer held in affection by the people of Norwich. The Magdalen Street flyover, when it was first proposed, did create a bit of a stir, to say the least! However, it removed a serious traffic bottleneck and residents now appreciate the benefits.

Another famous son of Norwich was born in 1504 in the parish of St Saviour's church. Mathew Parker was a vicar who was Master of Corpus Christi College in Cambridge. While briefly living in Norwich, he proved his bravery by attempting to preach to Kett's 20,000 rebel troops on Mousehold Heath in 1549. Worse the wear for drink, the troops began to heckle him and then turned very nasty, brandishing pikes and spears. He saw the error of his ways and rushed back to the safety of his home and then, on learning that they were planning to rob him the next day, he returned by devious means to Cambridge. He was to become Archbishop of Canterbury under

Gurney Court with the fine Georgian doorway to Elizabeth Fry's house.

Queen Elizabeth I and will be forever remembered by all practising clergymen for his thirty-nine statements of religious principles. A number of the rebels were tried and hung immediately from gallows by Magdalen Gates. Justice was carried out swiftly in these days.

Among the quality houses in this street was No. 10, which was the home of a wealthy merchant called Henry Thomas Martineau. This is where he brought up his children, Harriet and James, who were later to become famous. Harriet Marineau became a writer and campaigner for women's rights and James became a philosopher.

Opposite is a house in Gurney's Court, which was the home and original banking house of John Gurney. He subsequently moved his office to Bank Plain, where it became Barclays Bank. His famous daughter Elizabeth Fry, who campaigned for prison reform, was born in this house before Gurney set himself up in Earlham Hall to become a country squire.

An amusing story is told in Bethel Street police station, about what happened to a constable at Stumps Cross before dawn one snowy Christmas morning. The constable found to his amazement that in the middle of the road was a huge white rabbit sitting contentedly, adorned with a light covering of snow and totally oblivious to the festive season or the police interest. After double-checking that he was not seeing things, he rushed back to Magdalen Gates police station to obtain a wicker basket and captured a very relaxed rabbit. He traced the rabbit tracks in the snow back to an alley between terrace houses. Here he found a hutch in a garden with an open door, and he returned the rabbit to its home. By this time, the constable had wandered off his own beat and on the way back he met the Station Sergeant with an Inspector. They did not accept his explanation and insisted on being taken to the house to corroborate the story, silently creeping up to the hutch where they saw the rabbit. Had any member of the household looked out of the window at that moment looking for Santa Claus, they would have hurried back to bed to finish their dream.

Malthouse Road

At one time, Malthouse Road just a common lane or footpath. The road was developed in the nineteenth century when numerous malthouses were built in Norwich, creating a pleasant aroma over the city. Two malthouses were built here, one on each side of the road, hence the appropriate name.

Market Place

Mancroft was the original name of this marketplace, a name probably based on 'magna crofta', which means large croft or meadow. It was laid out after the Norman Conquest. The name survives in the St Peter Mancroft church to the south of the Market Place. Work started on this church in 1430 and it remains one of the jewels of Norwich (*see* St Peter's Street). For many generations, this was the French quarter of the city.

North of St Peter Mancroft is the church stile, where a snake reputed to be nearly fifty years old was on show in 1801. It was due to have a meal of 'quadrupeds' and adults were charged a shilling to watch it dine; poorer classes and children could watch the 9ft-long monster for half price.

It was not cheap to have a stall in Market Place. In 1841, the Corporation imposed annual tolls of £785 for a period of three years. There were some fascinating tradesmen's stalls in medieval times, including the following:

Bailey Market: situated next to the women's prison by the guildhall.

Cloutmarket: sold cloths, silks and linens.

Cobblers' Row: workshops and 'menders of shoes' on the east side, now Weavers Lane.

Cordwainers' Row: shoemakers at the north end of the market, by Gentlemen's Walk.

Hatters' Row: at the north end of the marketplace, now Guildhall Hill.

Murage Loft: where tolls for the stalls were collected. The name means 'a toll exacted for repairing walls' and there was plenty of this type of work to do in the city. It was located in the middle of Ironmongers' Row. The amount for each stall was set by the market committee, who met in the nearby guildhall.

Omanseterow: sellers of cloth made on a loom operated by one man, rather than that made on a broad loom worked by two people.

Scudders' Row: 'scudder' is a name peculiar to Norwich and refers to a 'dresser of white leather'. To 'scud' means 'to remove or cut remaining dirt or hairs from skins with a hand knife'.

Wastlemarket: wastel is bread made from the finest white flour. Bread was of suspicious quality until legislation brought it under control. It was given three headings: 'wastel bread', 'bread of wholewheat' and 'bread treet'.

Whittawers' Market: occupied by those who 'taws skins into whitleather', ready to be made into shoes, bags and the like.

Worsted Row: sold the famous Norfolk Cloth and yarn from the village of Worsted.

Fish market: now located in Mountergate.

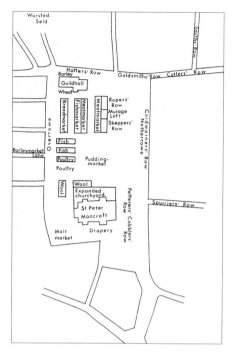

The approximate dimensions of rows in the marketplace during the fourteenth century, based on a draft by Helen Sutermeister.

A distressing part of the history of Market Place was the execution of rebels involved in Kett's Rebellion. Kett's men totalled approximately 2,500 to 3,000 and 300 of them were executed merely for fighting for justice and the education of their children. Forty-five met their death by being hung, drawn and quartered in Market Place. Many East Anglians may well find that their ancestors go back to those days, when Kett was supported by thousands of people from Dutch, Danish, German, Flemish, Huguenot and Saxon blood.

Stocks were placed in Market Place for men to spend an uncomfortable four or five hours of abuse and derision, which was the most common penalty for rowdy behaviour and drunkenness, though often a sentence was given just for a man speaking 'out of turn'. John Cobbe, a poor weaver, was put in the stocks for saying: 'The poor can buy no corn here for the rich churls take it from them', hardly a phrase worthy of such punishment. Stocks were not the only tools of the torturer's trade: there were also cages, ducking stools and whipping posts.

Arthur Orton, an ex-prisoner of Pentonville who was known as the 'Tichborne claimant', appeared in Sanger's Circus and would talk to the audience in Market Place about his life and adventures. An East London butcher weighing twenty-seven stones, he was the subject of one of the longest trials of the period, which lasted nearly two years. Lady Tichborne had advertised worldwide looking for her missing son and Orton convinced her that he really was Sir Roger Tichborne. Lady Tichborne died before the trial. Orton's case collapsed when an old school chum from Stonyhurst remembered that when he last saw Sir Roger, he weighed around nine stones, had the bearing of a guards officer and spoke with a Stonyhurst-educated accent. Not only that,

This lantern slide shows businesses, shops and horse-drawn vehicles in the eighteenth century.

Since it was created, the market square has been used for all kinds of assemblies. On this occasion it was so full that onlookers found their way onto the roof of the St Peter Mancroft church.

he had a tattoo on his left forearm. The trial came to a swift end and the jury took only thirty minutes to pronounce him guilty of perjury. He served fourteen years' hard labour before joining the circus.

Anti-German feeling was apparent in the city during the First World War, as rumours began to circulate about outrages committed by the Germans. Businesses and pubs with German-sounding names, such as the King of Prussia, were smashed and vulgar graffiti painted on their walls. Some German waiters from the Hotel De Paris in Cromer were brought to Norwich and placed in a barbed wire and wooden cage in the Market Place, guarded by troops with fixed bayonets.

The square now contains permanent stalls but until the 1930s the stalls were cleared away every week and the area could be used for gatherings and celebrations. Prior to the building of the new City Hall in 1938, most of the offices, pubs and hotels close to this area were demolished and the country market town image was lost forever. The whole market site is now being redesigned and most of the stalls will be replaced with modern structures, while keeping the character of the market. Many familiar stalls will be relocated and new open areas created, with seating for tired shoppers.

Mariners Lane

The lane was once called Hollegate, meaning 'street with a hollow', because there was a groove running through it created by a constant stream of surface water from Ber Street. The current name, which has been used since the eighteenth century, comes from the Three Mariners Inn.

Mountergate

These two roads have to be taken together because originally Mountergate was 'Inferior Conesford', which ran from Kings Street to Tombland. Eventually it was split by the new Prince of Wales Road, which then became known as St Faiths. This ancient lane, which dates back to the thirteenth century, has had too many name changes to mention. Some names were based on churches such as St Vedast's, or Faith's, that no longer exist. The name Mountergate derives from Parmentergate – a name also found in the church of St Peter Permountergate – a rectory in the patronage of Roger Bigod, who gave it to the Priory of Norwich. The monks rebuilt the church in the fifteenth century.

Muspole Street

The name of this street means a spring or pool. Perhaps the water was a little inferior, as the spelling suggests 'mouse' or 'moss pool' or may even be derived from the word 'must', meaning the juice of grapes. Sometimes it is found as the name of a river, denoting a 'muddy stream or pool'. Continuing on this theme, there was a medieval 'musspool' or cesspit at the southern end of the street.

The Walsingham priors had a town house in this street to accommodate their staff and to entertain guests when they visited Norwich. Until quite recently, the street was heavily industrialised. Seymour House and Lion House adjoined the huge Kiltie Shoe Factory and many of their workers actually lived in the street. At one time, part of the street was called Southgate. This was a corruption of Soutergate, from the cobblers' and shoemakers' trade. On the right is Alms Lane, which contained a number of almshouses that were rebuilt and converted into a boot factory in Victorian times. In 1977, the city council took them over and converted them into four dwellings.

N

New Mills Yard

The last time corn mills were operating here was in the fifteenth century but the name has stuck. This street crosses the river to Oak Street, where a waterworks took water from a conduit that continued serving the city until the end of the Victorian era.

A large number of Flemish refugees escaping persecution by the Spanish came to live in this area during the seventeenth century. They joined the Flemish-born weavers who were already settled in Norwich and whose specialised techniques enlivened local work practices. They were also proficient in breeding caged birds and were responsible for spreading this hobby throughout Europe, where canaries in particular were kept for their song. Georgian grandees treated the birds as fashionable accessories, so colour became an important factor. Attempts were made to establish a plumage that would rival the birds of paradise found in tropical regions. Birds were bred with huge feathers of different colours and they began to win shows. However, this craze was stopped as a result of a conference in London in 1890.

The weavers who had introduced the canary into the city saw the birds' popularity spread very quickly and, before long, thousands of Norwich people had dozens of cages in every available spare room in their house. Because of this pedigree and heritage, Norwich quickly became the centre of breeding and the bird became known as the Norwich canary. The original bird had natural striped plumage and bore no resemblance to the bright yellow we see today. It was also a different size. Only the skill of the Norwich fanciers has brought it to the level we have reached today. The poor bird, however, must have a strong constitution, for the colour was produced by experimentally feeding the birds with red beetroot, port wine, rape seed, carophyl and even hot spices – it's a wonder they didn't use Colman's mustard! They did try something

William Blake was a leading Norwich canary breeder.

equally spicy: tumeric and cayenne pepper. In Scotland, there is a variety of Norwich canary that is predominately red in colour. Perhaps it is only a matter of time before a tartan one appears! Canaries are difficult to identify as male or female; the easiest way is to hear them sing for only males have this ability. The yellow Norwich canary is the premier type at any show.

Ninhams Court

Originally called Masters Court, it was renamed after Henry Ninham who was born in 1793 at No. 10 Chapel Field. He was an artist of many skills, including sketching, oils and engraving, and was particularly noted for his intricate painting of coats of arms, so often seen on the coaches of titled families. He loved painting old buildings and his speciality was to do engraved individual plates of their doorways. This quiet court is well worth a visit and Henry's house in particular is simple but charming.

Oak Street

In the seventeenth century, this street had a mixture of buildings that suffered from floods, neglect, woodworm and dry rot. It came as no surprise when they were condemned and cleared away by the council. The population who lived here were rehoused in the city and factories took the place of domestic housing.

Floods did more damage in 1912 and took the life of local fish porter George Brodie, who was a real hero. He lived in this street and, although he suffered with asthma, this did not stop him from helping his friend Herbert Nixon wade through the chest-high raging torrents to find and carry women and children to safety. He ignored his wife's pleading for him to stop or at the least rest. It was difficult for the men to stay upright in the 30mph current and they lost their footing several times. They maintained contact by calling to each other until nearly midnight, when Brodie fell over and was washed away. Nixon thought that he had become tired and had gone home and it wasn't until the next day, when he was searching for him among friends, that he saw an ambulance carrying Brodie's body down King Street. Brodie's hands were crossed over his chest as though he had suffered a heart attack.

In the White Lion public house, which was originally called the Tap and Spittle, ghosts have been known to move bottles, glasses, and even tables. A former landlord was hung for murdering a prostitute who would not stay out of his pub, and it is thought that he returns now and again to ensure that the selling of food and drink is the only trade carried out here.

Opie Street

As the first red-light district of the city, it does no justice to the lady who gave her name to this street Amelia Opie. She was the daughter of a doctor and her father thought that the family was let down when she married John Opie, who was a divorcee and an artist, both of which were considered a lower class in those days. However, John became well known and painted a portrait of the great John Crome. Amelia wrote a number of books including *Father and Daughter* in 1801.

In the early nineteenth century, a sedan chair stood at the bottom of this sloping street, which was also known as The Devil's Alley. The street was originally a run of steep steps leading from Castle Meadow to London Street.

Orford Hill – Orford Place

Once the old Hog Market, this small space has a fascinating history. It was originally known as Hog Hill and was renamed after George Walpole, third Earl of Orford. Known as the 'Mad Earl', he spent his life pursuing pleasures of every description, instead of concentrating on the upkeep of Houghton Hall, the family seat. He loved all blood sports and tried to breed a fast type of greyhound. Gambling was another of his vices; he once had a bet with a friend that he could drive a flock of geese to London faster than his friend's turkeys. George knew that the turkeys would want to roost every night while his geese would keep going, so it was no contest. Later, he had to sell many priceless articles from the Hall to pay his various gambling debts. He was generous both in monetary terms and in giving his time to the city and the county, and he was proud of his appointment as Lord Lieutenant of Norfolk. In this position he was allowed to nominate the Member of Parliament for Castle Rising, so, cheekily, he chose a Whites Club billiard marker as the prospective MP. Having had dozens of affairs, when his favourite mistress died, Walpole had her body hidden in a boot cupboard. At the age of sixty-one, he fell from his horse while hunting and did not survive the injuries.

This important but small area forms a triangle where there were a number of individual shops, including Darlow's gun shop with its imposing stag put there by a Mr Jeffries, who was quite a colourful character. The original Victorian stag was replaced by a concrete one in 1970 and can still be seen. At the end of Red Lion Street, where it joins Farmers Avenue, is the Bell Hotel. This ancient hotel on Orford Hill was built in the sixteenth century. Some of its more colourful customers were known as members of the Hellfire Club, so-called because they loved blood sports such as cockfighting. Supposedly calling themselves gentlemen, they were just tough bullies intent on removing the Methodists and everything they stood for. Any preacher was fair game to them and Charles Wesley was a prime target when he came to Norwich in 1754. The hotel was known as the place where any revolutionary society could meet and plan their activities.

There were more serious activities that took place on Orford Hill. In 1876, the Church of England Young Men's Society (CEYMS) moved here with nearly 800 members. They studied music, singing, languages, architecture, mathematics, accounting and shorthand. Sports and recreation finally took over as the main occupation of the students.

The No. 10 tram ran from Orford Place to Silver Road. Mr G. Hill was the senior driver and is accompanied by the youngest employee, Mr B. Fisher.

Reverend William D'Oyley was an amazing eithteenth-century parson from Stratton St Michael who lived in Orford Place. With not a penny to his name, he rode his horse the equivalent of fifteen times the distance of Land's End to John O'Groats and was responsible for the widening of Orford Hill and many other streets in Norwich. Here was a man of action who was determined to make the roads of the city and Norfolk safer. On finding a hill or bend that was dangerous to negotiate, he would immediately get on his horse and ride to all the surrounding villages, raising money to pay for road improvements. On his death, he left £400 in his will for his lifetime's work to continue; the money was put into a trust fund and was put to use for another thirty-five years.

In the early 1900s, Orford Place was laid out as a tram terminus, with Curl's department store on its south side. In October 1933, the last tram ever to run in Norwich started from here, where the timekeeper's office and passengers' shelter were located. Throughout the final day, over 500 passengers crammed into the trams to enjoy the moment. Those seated upstairs constantly sang happy travelling songs such as 'Roll Along' and on the last tram this continued all the way to the terminus, where the mood changed to one of sadness and 'Auld Lang Syne' was sung.

Even with one broken antler, this stag on what was originally Darlow's gun shop is still imposing and looks down on all those below him.

The Bell Hotel in the 1890s. Note the trader's handcart outside.

There was a lot of bomb damage in 1940 but luckily the Bell Hotel and the castle were left virtually unscathed.

Heavy bombing devastated the whole area in 1942. One bomb made a crater so large that it was used as a static water tank. An American serviceman who wanted a bath, or maybe did it for a wager, actually swam across it, to the delight of onlookers cheering him on. After the war, many plans were put forward including one to create a large civic square with a central traffic island. Curl's, now Debenhams, won the day and built a new store in 1955, which split the old Orford Place and changed the streets beyond recognition.

P

Palace Street

Originally this street was called White Horse Street, after a popular local inn of that name. Fights and scuffles regularly took place here, particularly in the turbulent days of Kett's Rebellion. As the

Bussey's Garage has now been closed and the site is being developed.

street runs through to St Martin's Plain, adjacent to the Bishop's Palace, it comes as no surprise that the street name was changed to the more appropriate Palace Street.

Bussey's Garage, once known as Bussey & Sabberton, has been closed down for redevelopment into a riverside housing project. In his youth, Mr Charles Bussey once climbed to the top of the spire of Norwich Cathedral with some friends, making good use of the scaffolding in place while it was undergoing renovation.

Pigg Lane

Situated off Palace Street, it was first called Wateryne Lane; the name then changed many times according to its most important resident. It's current name is a reference to Henry Pigge, the city's Chief Constable in 1514.

Pottergate

This street used to extended from outside the city walls all the way to London Street but is now split into three roads: Pottergate, Lobster Lane and Bedford Street. Remains of early earthenware and pottery dating back to Saxon times have been found in the area but by the thirteenth century there were no potteries left in Norwich. The history of this trade is preserved by the street name.

At the western end is a fine house where Joseph Kinghorn, a scholar and divine, lived. He was a minister of St Mary's Baptist church from 1789 to 1832. The huge building on the north side of the street by Piper Whalley & Partners was aptly named Kiln House. Other industries prevailed here in the eighteenth century; silk and shoe manufacturing in particular. Borrow House was named after George Borrow, the author of *Lavengro* and *Romany Rye*, who lived here for some time.

Sir Benjamin Wrench also had a house here. Wrench's Court to the rear of the house was named after him and was for some while the location of the Norwich Society. It later became the New Lobster Inn, whose landlord was proud of the fact that 'the North Pole is in a direct line from this spot'.

There used to be an eye infirmary here, founded by three wealthy gentlemen. It had moved from St Benedict's Plain into bigger premises and was a charity for around a dozen inpatients and over 400 outpatients. It became so busy that it was constantly expanding and, as a result, was finally incorporated into the Norfolk and Norwich Hospital.

In this road stood the Infirmary for Sick Children, founded in 1853 by the Swedish opera singer Johanna or Jenny Lind. It is hard to explain the worldwide success of this singer: she received the kind of adulation that is now given to the greatest of film stars. When she came to Norwich, the city was brought to a standstill, even though probably there was not one person there who had heard her sing because there was no media in those days. The church leader Bishop Stanley entertained her, much to the chargrin of the 'county set'. He made a distinct impression on Jenny Lind and it was he who steered her to charity giving, which she took on with fervour. Once, he had to stop her making an extreme decision to give handfuls of money away to people in the marketplace. The nation went into mourning when she died in 1870. After the original hospital was relocated, the grounds were kept open as a children's play area until the 1960s. Her reputation has lived on in the Jenny Lind children's ward in the Norfolk and Norwich Hospital.

John George Foster, who lived at No. 60 Pottergate, killed Alice Maria Newby after an argument in their home. He was found guilty of manslaughter on 8 December 1897 and spent his life in penal servitude.

Right: *The gates of the Jenny Lind playground at Pottergate in 1965.*

Opposite above: *A view of Prince of Wales Road, in the 1930s.*

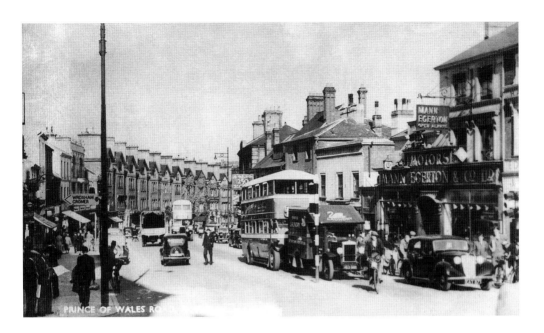

Prince of Wales Road

In 1859, the city council decided to construct this road by private investment. It seemed like a good idea at the time and the newly formed Norwich New Street Company was formed. It was their intention to build a road 500 yards long and 108ft wide from the station to Castle Meadow. They started by erecting some excellent buildings, until the money ran out. These elegant Georgian and Victorian properties were overlooked by other good examples of the style at that time: the Agricultural Hall, now home to Anglia Television, and the Royal Hotel.

Trains had grown into an important mode of transport; realising this, the council took over and built a larger road which went over the Wensum at Foundry Bridge and led to Thorpe railway station. Although it is on the east side of the Wensum, the station is worth a mention as a fine structure rebuilt in the latter part of the nineteenth century, which has recently been cleaned and redecorated. Foundry Bridge was first made of wood and then rebuilt with ornate ironwork in the 1880s, complementing the station.

Wales Square, on the north side of the road, once contained a number of Victorian houses but they were pulled down in the 1970s. After the Second World War, small groups of teenagers used to roam up and down the road, desiring to be part of the bustling scene even though they could only afford to have beans on toast or fish and chips in a café and maybe pop in to one of the two cinemas, the Regent and the Norvic. At that time there were no foreign restaurants but this all changed when the first oriental restaurant arrived, and the road is now full of every type of restaurant, as well as bustling nightclubs and pubs. It is a mecca for all those with the energy and appetite to enjoy nightlife to the full.

Princes Street

This street runs from the old Dominican friary at Hall Plain to Tombland. It was once known as Hundegate, a name derived from the Old English word 'hund' meaning hound, because the bishop's hounds were kept in kennels there. The name lives on in the church of St Peter Hungate on Elm Hill, which was rebuilt in 1460 by John and Margaret Paston and later became a museum of ecclesiastical art. The present street name comes from the Prince Inn.

Pudding Lane

Similar to the two Pudding Lanes in London, this street in the market was where puddings – entrails and who know what else stuffed into pig's intestines, as a kind of sausage – were sold from the fifteenth century.

Q

Queen Street

Constantly used as a shortcut to avoid the traffic lights, this road is very busy. The commuters dashing through probably miss the points of interest, such as the French Church in Old Bank of England Court. For 500 years, this was the church of St Mary the Less. It was later turned into a hall and used for varied purposes, such as the sale of yarn. It then reverted back to a church and was used over a long period by different denominations. It was also turned into a retail store at one stage.

Also in Old Bank of England Court is the attractive office of architect Edward Boardman, which has an ornate red-brick façade and a Victorian tiled entrance porch in excellent condition. The Bank of England had a branch here, one of many located across the country. In this building, the Norfolk and Norwich Arts Circle met for 100 years. They held their first exhibition on 12 September 1885.

Queens Road

This was once known as Brazen Doors Road, after the city gate situated at the junction with Grove Road, built, like many of the city wall fortifications, with money provided by Richard Spynke out of his own pocket. Queens Road joins the Inner Link Road. Halfway along the southern side, at the junction with Hall Road, is a public house named after William Cullum. Cullum was a showman who was better known as Billie Bluelight, an old name for a teetotaller. This well-built athlete sold items such as heather and wild flowers but he was better known for running races against wherry boats. He famously raced the *Jenny Lind* steamboat, and the *Yarmouth Belle* from Foundry Bridge in Norwich to Yarmouth.

R

Rampant Horse Street

The city's horse market was once held here and the street was called Horsemarket. The thirteenth-century Rampant Horse Inn stood on the north side of the street, taking its name from the market. It was famous for its 'learned pig' that could spell or count – depending on how much ale the customers had drunk. Even Parson Woodforde paid money to witness the phenomenon. The inn became notorious for the number of trunks shipped from its premises to London on the Telegraph coach. A porter delivered a trunk to the coach office which aroused suspicion and it turned out to contain a naked body of a man who had been buried two days earlier. The Reverend George Carter identified it, and two men named Collins and Crowe were subsequently sentenced to three months' imprisonment and fined £50 for bodysnatching. The inn closed down in around 1900.

In the 1930s, elaborate plans were under consideration by the city planners to dramatically alter this popular shopping area. There were several established retail outlets such as Curl Brothers – one of the first department stores in Norwich – Curry's, Timpson's and the Army and Navy Stores. Their removal would have created uproar and, luckily, the controversial plan was put on ice when German bombers, in one particular raid in April 1942, demolished the whole area.

Damage caused by the air raids of 1942 in Rampant Horse Street.

The Walnut Tree Shades public house, just off Gentleman's Walk in Old Post Office Yard.

St Stephen's church was built before the Norman Conquest; its porch dates from 1350. In the vestry is a painted alabaster tablet of nine saints and there are fine brasses, including those to Robert Brasyer, mayor in 1513. The east window contains old German glass.

In nearby St Stephen's Church Lane, which ran off the south side of this street adjacent to the church, there were several individual small shops. These, and other larger firms such as Boots and the Co-op, were destroyed by fires that followed the air raid.

The landlord of the Walnut Tree Shades was known to walk his dog in this area and often met his friend the local policeman, both of them having finished a tiring evening and nightshift duty. A treat of brown ale left by the landlord in a hiding place was quite refreshing to the constable, who took it to the unlocked St Stephen's church, where it was swigged down in peace and solitude. On one occasion, a constable was showing a new recruit this perk of the job and the recruit revealed that, in a strange coincidence, his great-great-grandfather, who was in the police force in 1884, was admonished for seeking a glass of ale in nearby Gentleman's Walk.

Recorder Road

Starting from St Faith's Lane, Recorder Road runs towards the river but turns sharp right before reaching it and continues to the Prince of Wales Road. The name suggests that in the past there was a connection with the holder of the office of City Recorder.

This street is a little jewel, which remains unknown to most people whether they are local or not. It is well worth viewing on foot as there are many buildings of interest, from the old vinegar works to the Christian Scientist church. There is also a delightful small park called the James Stuart Garden, which is a memorial to a Scot who was a great benefactor to the city.

Red Lion Street

The name is taken from an eighteenth-century inn that was serving customers until 1845. For some reason, this street was not shown on the Ordnance Survey map of 1885.

Redwell Street

There was a pump over a medieval well at the place where this street meets Bank Plain, hence it was called Red Well Street. In the late eighteenth century, the street was widened by 8ft.

The church of St-Michael-at-Plea, once called St Michael at Notstone, is so called because the Archdeacon of Norwich held his pleas, or courts, in the building. The lords of the manors of Sprowston and Horsford were patrons of the church and in the eighteenth century it was kept going with £600 of Queen Anne's Bounty. It has a nice clock dated 1827 on its tower with an inscription 'forget-me-not'. It's origins are unknown to the café/bookshop owners who have adopted this as a trading title. There are details of St George and the dragon over the porch entrance. The church contained painted panels now made into a reredos and there is also a brass dedicated to Barbara Ferrer, dated 1588, and a nave roof. At present, the church is being put to good use as a bookshop and a pleasant restaurant.

In October 1752, a Norwich smuggler called Mr Eager posed as a watchman and seized a sack containing 26lbs of tea. On his way home, two horsemen tried to snatch the sack but he held onto it, shouting at the top of his voice, and this forced them to retreat. Two hours later, the tea were taken from the Eagers' house. Mr Eager was sentenced and died later in Newgate prison.

The forget-me-not clock of St-Michael-at-Plea.

Rigbys Court

A tiny lane that connects Bethel Street to St Giles Street, Rigbys Court was called Pit Lane in the eighteenth century, a name which referred to a refuse pit that was filled in when the road was built. Dr Edward Rigby was the doctor who brought vaccination to Norwich while working in his own small smallpox hospital. He was also renowned for advances in gallstone surgery. This street was named after him as a memorial from a very grateful city, who presented him with an inscribed silver breadbasket. He made good use of this, and it was more often than not filled to the brim, for he had a large number of mouths to feed at home: twelve children including quadruplets.

River Lane

In times gone by, this lane led from Barrack Street to a landing stage on the River Wensum but there is no longer any access.

Riverside Road

Once a sheltered and busy towpath by the Wensum, this was an important commercial route. It is now part of the Inner Ring Road from Bishops Bridge Road to Koblenz Avenue. Early pirates named the river 'Wendsome', because of its torturous route through the city. They stopped here because they were unable to sail their boats any further than Cowgate. More lawful trade brought to the city by the river proved to be extremely valuable to Norwich. This road was a busy highway, bringing the materials used to build the castle and the cathedral. It was also a natural defence along the northern and eastern sides of the city.

A constable at Foundry Bridge was after a boy who had set all the boats adrift from the yacht station but the juvenile was sitting on a bicycle a few hundred yards down Riverside Road, cheerfully watching the boats float away. There was no way the constable could reach the boy undetected so he hitched a lift in a passing milk float and used the element of surprise to capture the boy.

Rosary Lane

Though not strictly within the boundaries of the city wall, this lane has been included because the nearby Nonconformist cemetery is the resting place of one of the greatest men of Norwich: mustard producer Jeremiah James Colman, who died in September 1898.

Opposite Bishops Bridge is a plot of land enclosed by trees, which is called the Nest. It includes Norwich City football club's first ground, before it relocated to Carrow Road in 1935.

Rose Lane

Like so many roads, Rose Lane is named after a public house. It takes its name from the Rose Tavern, which dated from 1688 but no longer exists. The lane spans the River Wensum at

The Canaries have come a long way since they played here in the 1930s.

Foundry Bridge, erected in around 1800. It was the only road linking the city to the railway station at Thorpe and now leads into the fairly new Prince of Wales Road. There have been three bridges at this site; the first was a toll bridge.

Rosemary Lane

Here we have Pilgrims Hall, a fifteenth-century building that escaped the great fire that devastated the area in 1507. It is situated at the north end of the lane and was also known as Pykerell's House, as it was once the home of three times mayor, Thomas Pykerell. In Tudor times, it had a queen-post thatched roof. It was later converted into an inn named the Rosemary Tavern, and this gave the street its name.

Once densely populated with many alleys and courtyards and gabled Victorian houses, this picturesque lane became one of the worst slum areas of Norwich. Fortunately it was included in one of the early slum clearance schemes of the 1920s.

The lane leads into St Miles Alley, which is on one side of a triangle of land housing the church of St Michael Coslany, now a gift shop and discovery centre.

Rouen Road

Following the route of many old streets, this is a modern road named after Norwich's twin town of Rouen in France. St Martin's church was situated here, very close to the castle, and all who met their fate in the castle precincts were buried in the graveyard. This task was transferred to St-Michael-at-Thorn church (*see* Thorn Street). The modern Eastern Counties Newspapers building has a plaque on its walls denoting the site of the church. Their large headquarters bears little relationship to offices they originally had in London and Redwell Streets. Perched on a hill and illuminated at night, it has become a landmark and, with its myriad publications, it is now considered to be a leading centre of modern communications.

Royal Arcade – one could be forgiven for imagining this is an entrance to a kasbah.

Royal Arcade

Connecting Gentleman's Walk to Arcade Street, this is a privately owned route from the castle to the city market. Famous architect George Skipper made his name from the design of this Edwardian masterpiece. Born the son of a builder in Dereham, Skipper went to the Bracondale School and the Norwich School of Art. After a period of training as an architect in London, he eventually opened a business in Norwich. Having made his mark by designing the Paris, Metropole and Grand Hotels in Cromer, he started on the Royal Arcade, which was completed in 1899. From its bird-covered Doulton tiles to the tree-patterned stained-glass windows, and not forgetting its Moorish arches which prompted Pevsner to say 'it's innocent in the front but very naughty when its back is turned', it was, and still is, a constant source of pride to the people of Norwich. Skipper's vivid imagination is let loose on so many buildings throughout the city. His use of statues and multicoloured bricks and tiles made him unique. When he died in 1948, at the age of ninety-two, his firm went on to build many other excellent properties that are easily identifiable. These outshine the monotonous modern premises that prevail in the city.

S

St Andrew's Hill

Named after St Andrew's church, this road runs from St Andrew's Street to Bedford Street. It used to be a long flight of steps called Seven Steps but these were removed in 1761. A committee was set up to discuss the widening and enlarging of the street, which took place in1762. One of the best examples in the city of 'squared' knapped flint can be seen on the walls of St Andrew's church.

A popular city eccentric named Charles Archer died near here on 19 November 1820, aged eighty-one. It was his duty to be at his post near the Two-Necked Inn every morning at four o'clock with his kettle of hot cocoa. He was given half a pint of porter if he woke the landlord up at six o'clock in the morning. He valiantly did this every day for fourteen years, consuming 2,556 half pints of the ale. He had been in the 12th Foot Regiment and lost a leg in the Siege of Gibraltar, for which he was granted a pension for the rest of his life. This terrible injury was bad enough but, as he often related to people, insult was added when a hog snatched the dismembered limb in his mouth and ran away with it! There is no doubt this is what affected Archer's mind.

St Andrew's Plain

Here we have St Andrew's Hall, built on land once owned by a small religious order called the Friars of de Sacco. Their original building had been destroyed by a fire that killed two of the friars. The current building was the nave of the Black Friars' conventional church, acquired on behalf of

 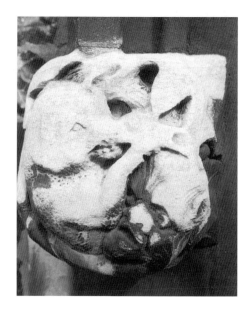

Top: *Extraordinary flint work abounds on St Andrew's Hall.*

Above left and right: *Look closely and the pigs will reveal themselves, south porch, St Andrew's Hall.*

the Norwich Corporation in 1541 by future mayor Augustine Steward. In 1853, the new cult of 'table turning' or spiritualism was introduced for the first time in Norwich when Mr King gave a séance at St Andrews Hall.

The adjacent Blackfriars Hall was the chancel of the friary church favoured by the city's Dutch congregation. Thousands of Flemish Protestants sought refuge here to escape persecution from the Duke of Alva. As a result, their well-known skills in weaving processes came to the city, which greatly improved local techniques and benefited the trade. There used to be a tall octagonal tower over the walkway that separates the two halls but this collapsed in 1712. Many and varied activities have taken place here: it has been used as courtroom, granary, municipal chapel, library, artillery and mint. Functions of every kind, from beer festivals to Masonic meetings and animal shows, have been held in the hall over the past 400 years. It was the usual custom for incoming mayors to hold a banquet and many used the hall. In 1561, it cost the mayor an enormous £1 18s 1d. In today's money, they were paying 6p for eight pints of beer, 10p for four brace of partridges, 1p for sixteen oranges and 25p for eight stones of prime beef! An extensive corn market was held in the hall from 1796 until 1828, when it was removed to the Corn Exchange in Exchange Street.

On 4 November 1851, a huge audience of young men, under the pretence of being shop assistants and milliner's apprentices, crammed into the Hall to see and hear a widely publicised lecture on Bloomer Costume given by Mrs Knights. Expecting to see a saucy display of fashion, they were bitterly disappointed when Mrs Knights came onstage in an ugly and unfeminine dress known as a 'bloomer', considered ideal for ladies' outdoor pursuits such as bicycling and riding. She was greeted with howls of laughter, catcalls, whistling and derision and rushed off the stage, leaving the orchestra to face a bombardment of groans.

Controversy raged after the City Surveyor, an Irishman named Thomas Barry, 'restored' St Andrew's Hall in 1863. The west front was his own design, as was the south porch. This particularly upset the *Norwich Mercury*:

The needless, utterly useless Porch, perishing to the audience while in the Hall with the cutting draught, and more destructive when they come out cold, comfortless, miserable in its nakedness, and bare walls, with its open external portal, its iron gates preventing shivering females from seeking the only refuge in these corners – its end will come… This offspring of false taste and false statement, except that it is the true child of such parents, neither useful nor ornamental, deformed and misshapen, its life can be but one of suffering – its last moment will be the happiest, the blithest of its existence… The inhabitants of the Emerald Isle are so imaginative, it is said, and so unstable, that to blunder and mistake is their nature. Would it not be a wonder then, if the Surveyor of the City was different from his countrymen.

However, the surveyor had a sense of humour: the *Mercury* editor's name was Bacon and, if you look closely at the stonework of the south porch, there are four pigs. One is blowing his own trumpet, another is playing an organ to smiling demons, the third pig is disgorging reptiles with a devil sucking out his brains and the last pig is gulping down the west front before a group of devils.

Built with timber from a sixteenth-century Armada galleon, this part of Garsett House was well worth saving.

St Andrew's Street

For over 100 years, this road was called Wymer's Street. Wymer was the name of one of the medieval leets – a record of an area which contains certain manors that had jurisdiction over them – of Norwich. In ancient times Wymerus is recorded as being a follower of William de Warren and a steward of his estates in Norfolk.

Once full of beautiful gabled houses, the street soon echoed to the sound of horse-drawn carts with iron-rimmed wheels and was lined with straw to deaden the noise. Not to be outdone by a mode of transport used in other parts of the city, in the late nineteenth century the road was cut wider to accommodate the new noisy trams, which also ran on iron wheels and rails. Many fine buildings, including the City Arms public house and part of the sixteenth-century Garsett House, had to be demolished. Fortunately, a small part of the original Garsett House building was retained. It incorporates a frame said to have come from an Armada galleon of 1589, which was wrecked off the Norfolk coast. It may now look a little strange but it was worth saving.

Cinema City was purchased by the council in 1924 and turned into a cinema in 1979. The building dates back to 1285. It was an early Tudor merchant's home known as Suckling House, after Robert Suckling who was mayor in 1572 and 1582. It was once owned by the Colman family, who gave it to the city in 1924, and it was the location of the first ever Round Table meeting in 1927.

Sir John and Lady Suckling have a large canopied tomb in nearby St Andrew's, a church that was enlarged in the fifteenth century. The tomb depicts his wife beside him and a son kneeling at each end, with their four sisters kneeling in prayer on the front. They were forbears of Lord Nelson, who was a pupil at Norwich Grammar School and regularly attended this church.

In March 1943, the clothing factory of F.W. Harmer was burned to the ground during the worst bombing raid of that year and two of their workers were badly injured. Shortly afterwards, St Andrew's church was hit, together with a nearby baker's shop, estate agent and restaurant. This church, with 96ft-high tower that luckily escaped damage, is the second largest church in the city, and is an excellent medieval structure.

St Ann Lane

St Ann Lane is based on a derivation of St Anthony's Lane of 1696. Smugglers who did not want to risk entering Norwich through one of the twelve gates often made good use of the river Wensum. On a dark night in June 1779, they tried to smuggle in several half-ankers of gin. An anker is measure of liquid used when trading with Holland; at this time, an anker tub held 10 gallons. Shipped across the North Sea, the gin was so strong and over-proof, that over 2 gallons of water had to be added to it, which made it even more profitable. Space was always left in the tubs to improve their buoyancy in case they had to be thrown overboard. Smugglers around the Norfolk coasts and on rivers and broads also used another method: they weighted tubs with

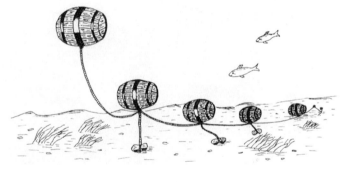

A method used by smugglers to sink a crop of tubs containing spirits on the seabed.

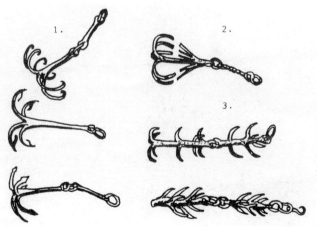

Creepers were dragged along the seabed to bring sunken contraband to the surface.

Once on land, the tubs were carried over the shoulder or over the back of a pony.

sinking stones and dumped them overboard, attached to a recovery line. The other end of the line was fixed to a buoy just below the surface. This method of hiding the contraband was known as 'sowing the crop'. When the coast was clear, the tubs could be collected. Tying up their boat at St Ann's Staithe, the smugglers were just about to land the tubs when some officers who had been hiding nearby jumped into the boat and siezed the cargo.

Not all contraband was for local use: in 1783, the York stagecoach was found to have over 1cwt of tea and some gin hidden aboard. After a tip-off received by the Excise Office in Tombland, it was seized by a party of dragoons near Thetford.

St Augustine's

In the period between 1300 and 1700, several outbreaks of the Black Death caused panic in the city. Locking the gates as soon as word reached Norwich that there had been an outbreak nearby failed to keep the plague out. Sick people were taken by wheelbarrow to a pest house in St Benedict's that quickly became full and soon this area was also riddled with plague. Houses that were infected were daubed with a white cross, and dogs, cats and even hogs were hunted down and destroyed in case they were carriers. A huge pest house in St Augustine's was enlarged further to take more victims and before the Black Death finally left Norwich in 1667, nearly 2,500 people had died and were buried in pits outside the city walls.

On 7 January 1701, hard-drinking man and weaver Robert 'Gaffer' Watts was in his local, the Globe, and took the bait from a friend who was well aware of Gaffer's jealous nature. The friend claimed that he had bedded Watts' wife and said 'there isn't much from me she wouldn't stand

– I'd get the wedding ring from off her hand'. The wager was a gallon of beer and the so-called friend went to see the wife. He told her that the ring was required by her husband to settle a bet and the poor lady, nervous of Gaffer's temper, gave the man the ring, which he waved in front of Watts. Before hearing that it was all a joke, he stormed to his house and repeatedly stabbed his wife with a knife:

> *Trembling and bleeding, up again she flies,*
> *Unto the window, where she vainly tries,*
> *To call assistance; but no help was near.*
> *And so he cut her throat from ear to ear.*
> (From Neil Storey's *A Grim Almanac of Norfolk*)

Gaffer was executed in front of his own house on 30 August 1701.

St Benedict's

This important area of the city is steeped in history. It was once known as Westwick, one of the four original hamlets that probably formed the city of Norwich in the nineteenth century. The street is on the route of the early Saxon east-west road across the county. It was a wealthy area based on the woollen trade, a fact which is confirmed by the large number of churches in the proximity. There was a beautiful fourteenth-century castellated gate at the western end of the

A reproduction of St Benedict's Gate, taken from a sketch.

street called St Benedict's Gate. This is where the Earl of Warwick, with his German mercenaries, entered the city to finally put down Kett's Rebellion. There were 20,000 rebels running riot, raiding and firing buildings (*see* Tombland). In quieter times, pilgrims on their way to the shrine at Walsingham regularly passed through and it became known as Heaven's Gate. Unfortunately, this was demolished in 1793 as the road became busier and it was later turned into one of the most popular city shopping areas. There used to be a wonderful square or plain here that extended across to Pottergate, surrounded by a very smart group of houses dating from the sixteenth century, of which only a few remain. The rest were demolished by the city council to make way for a proposed new road, which never came about as the Second World War intervened.

A crowd celebrating Christmas Eve in 1899 had their party in a café cut short by Horace Alfred Cox who, maybe a jealous lover, fired three shots at Ellen Parker and, missing her completely, turned the gun on himself. He died shortly afterwards in the Norfolk and Norwich Hospital.

Although air traffic is increasing at Norwich airport, planes still attract attention when flying over the city. This was not the case during the Second World War, when the population were used to seeing the skies black with planes going to and from local RAF and USAAF stations or enemy bombers on their way to towns such as Coventry. Used to the sight of formations of aeroplanes and the subsequent sirens that heralded their arrival, they hardly warranted a second glance from the population. Apart from in a few isolated instances, people did not even seek cover in air-raid shelters.

This calm attitude changed on 27 April 1940, after the area was flattened in a heavy bombing raid. Prior to this extensive damage, any strangers to the city could be shown a piece of the original St Benedict's Gate hinge pin, still visible in part of the remains of the city wall. Following the worst bombing of the war, residents understood the meaning of the word 'blitz'. Those who survived quickly moved out and, through the resulting loss of trade, neglect set in and businesses closed down. The Inner Ring Road brought relief from the through-traffic in 1975 and subsequent reconstruction and development, as well as restoration, has greatly improved the area.

The lack of sufficient numbers of worshippers has seen St Margaret's church put to an entirely different use as a health club, changing from spiritual health to bodily health. A short distance along the road, still on the north side, is another much larger redundant church, St Lawrence's. Unusually for Norfolk, this church has a battlemented tower with an unusual spirelet on its northeast corner, which dates from the 1890s. When the road was widened, much of the churchyard was obliterated. Next door to the church are large buildings once occupied by Bullard's Brewery, one of four leading brewers of the city. It was taken over by Watney's, who then closed it – one way of getting rid of the opposition. The premises were derelict for a while but, with the help of grant aid, it is now a housing and office complex.

St Catherine's Close

Situated just off Surrey Street, this street has one of the most beautiful houses in Norwich. It was built by John Morse when he became Sheriff in 1779 and he lived here for fifty years. One of his favourite drinks was porter and he brewed this himself. He was not bothered that this drink was considered mainly for the lower classes, especially market porters, from where the name originated. The house used to be occupied by the BBC but at the time of writing it is up for sale.

St Catherine's Plain

The Inner Ring Road has taken its toll here, reducing the plain to a small patch of shrubs and grass. In the early eighteenth century, there was a thriving community here and many trades, which included bakers, drapers, tea makers and wheelwrights. They were refreshed by three local inns. There was a church dedicated to St Catherine, which fell into disrepair. Most of the residents of the plain died as a result of the Black Death in the fourteenth century and it never recovered. Demolition followed and the only thing to be seen now is a street sign, and a reference to the name on the office of the BBC at All Saints Green.

St Crispin's Road

St Crispin is the patron saint of the shoemaking trade that used to abound in Norwich. Out of all the many churches in Norwich, none are dedicated to this saint. This road is quite a modern addition to the city's infrastructure and forms part of the Inner Ring Road.

The phenomenal artist, composer and musician William Crotch was born in this parish. With a name like that, it comes as no surprise that he was interested in crotchets and quavers at eighteen months old. He played Mozart two years later and performed before royalty. Crowds used to gather outside his house to listen to the child when he was practising. At twenty-two, he became a professor of music at Oxford and first principal of the Royal Academy of Music at forty-seven. Although he went on to teach for fifty years, he had to resign from the Academy because he was caught in the act of kissing and cuddling a girl student. His paintings are well known but his music less so, apart from the Westminster Chimes heard on the radio and used in many clocks.

At the eastern end of this road, where it meets Barrack Street, is a roundabout on the site of the church of St Paul. This fine old round-towered building dating back to the Norman Conquest stood for centuries until suffering severe war damage in 1942. It was never repaired and remained as a ruin until this part of the Inner Ring Road was built.

St Faith's Lane

Norwich weavers were sometimes overzealous in defending their trade. A riot took place over two days in protest against the Court of Guardians relief committee, who had authorised that two looms should be erected in the workhouse. Richard Knockolds took it upon himself to throw sulphuric acid in the face of John Wright, a principal master manufacturer of St Faith's Lane. Knockolds was outwardly a family man who had five children, though he had been known to travel out into the countryside and set fire to haystacks, barns and farms for no logical reason.

His family and friends attended his trial, as did hundreds of onlookers who were so bemused by the actions he was unable to explain. He was contrite in court and received sympathy from the crowds. The judge, however, had no qualms in sending him to the gallows and, when he dropped, total silence fell on the local population who had thronged to the Castle Ditches to witness this event.

St George's Plain

The large base of this triangular piece of land fronts onto Colegate but even so the area is still known as St George's Plain. The church of St George goes back to the eleventh century and has a carving of the saint and dragon in a niche on the south side of the chancel. There is a brass to an aptly named mayor of 1461, William Norwyche, and his wife and son.

St George's Street

This is another street that has been split by the Inner Ring Road. The old Botolph Street is now merely a footpath leading to Anglia Square, known as Botolph Way. The original street ran from St Augustine's to St George's, ending at the junction with Colegate.

The attractive bridge over the Wensum called St George's Bridge or Blackfriars Bridge was built in 1784, on the site of an earlier medieval structure that was designed by Sir John Soane, an architect to the Bank of England. Norwich would have done well to use his contacts at the bank for some funding, as money to build roads and bridges had to come from revenue obtained from tolls on cargoes travelling upriver. These proved enough to build bridges but left little for the maintenance of the roads leading to them.

At the southern end is the Norwich Art School, on the site of a medieval brewhouse. It was founded by Old John Crome, after he married Phoebe Berney in 1792. He lived in a house close by in Green Lane. They had a daughter named Abigail, who unfortunately lived for only two years. Later they went on to have two daughters and five sons, one of which turned out to be a fine painter. He was also called John Crome, so his father came to be known as Old Crome to save any confusion.

Nearby is a quadrangle known as the Garth. It was formerly a cloister, part of the precincts surrounding the church of the Dominican or Black Friars when they moved here from Colegate. Prior to the Art School, the King Edward VI School was housed here. The monastery chapel nearby was used by the fascinating and deeply religious Victorian preacher Father Ignatious. Here was a man of self-confessed divine destiny, who saw a ghost when he was only seven years old. He suffered severe shock at St Paul's School in London after receiving forty lashes for studying a book on the Holy Land instead of a textbook. He took holy orders in Scotland and became a monk on his own account, with two other men joining him later. His second order took him to Suffolk and his third to Norwich, where he opened Elm Hill House as a monastery. He had many converts even though the regime was extremely strict and the monks lived on bread, water and potatoes and said prayers eight times a day – although Ignatious did not observe this himself. It is said that he performed miracles and anyone who upset or cursed him suddenly became ill or died. His punishments for transgressors were legendary, from caning to drawing an outline of the cross on the floor with one's tongue. He carried on around the country for over forty years and there were riots in London every time he preached. He ended up founding a monastery in the Brecon Beacon mountains of Wales.

Giovanni Bianchi had a business here. He was a figure maker in the early nineteenth century and one day was called to the castle to make a death mask for the most notorious murderer that ever walked the streets of Norwich: James Blomfield Rush. Known as 'the double murderer' for killing the Recorder of Norwich and his son, it is said that he once even tried to kill his own mother. Trains brought people from all over the country to see him on the day of his public execution and 22,000 people crowded into the bailey of the castle. His death mask can be seen today in Norwich Castle.

On the evening of Friday 8 March 1918, a motley group of about thirty Norwich boys stood outside an old building in St George's Street, anxiously waiting for the doors to be opened so that they could see what the Norwich Lads' Club had to offer. They had no idea that from this first day, a movement would be created that would spread across Britain and every corner of the globe. The boys had been drawn there by leaflets signed by Richard Jewson, Lord Mayor of Norwich. E.J. Caley was president and then became its first chairman. Generous gifts and cash donations from city firms and individuals made it possible for this to be a mini paradise for boys between the ages of fourteen and eighteen, most of whom had been brought up in needy and drab homes during the First World War which was drawing to an end. The founder of the club was John Henry Dam,

The interior of the Lads' Club, showing the leisure activities on offer.

a revolutionary Chief Constable of Norwich. This example of his rhetoric is taken from a speech he made to the Norwich Rotary Club in 1926: 'Too many parents tie up a dog at night and turn the boy loose to run at will'.

Dam's advocacy of 'manly pursuits' led to the magnificent tradition of boxing, which is still enjoyed by the club. The activities have changed to keep up with the times and now girls are admitted and age limits loosely interpreted. Throughout its history, many people have given devoted service to the Lads' Club but it survives as a monument to an inspired idealistic policeman who, when he opened the door of his club in St George's Street in 1918, also opened the door to a whole new world for thousands of youngsters.

St Giles' Street

Dr Edward Rigby, founder of the Norfolk and Norwich Hospital, lived here in the eighteenth century. He had an interest in smallpox and mental illness and introduced vaccination into the city. At the same time, he was treating twelve lunatics in a house at Lavenham. Being a man of action, he spent some time in Paris during the French Revolution, also mixing with the rebels on their return from storming the Bastille. At a farm in Framlingham Earl, Rigby grew herbs for experimental medicine, including opium poppies. Plants were grown to assist fertilisation and as his wife bore twelve children, including quadruplets, they seem to have worked. He loved trees and was responsible for convincing the city council to plant large quantities of them. He even kicked out some of his tenants so that he could demolish their houses and plant even more trees.

Dr Rigby designed an outside toilet that was better than anything designed by the famous Mr Crapper. Encircled by trees, this landscaped unit collected rainwater for flushing purposes and the stored water drained into a pond in which he grew watercress. It is not recorded whether the taste was tainted in view of the source but his wife loved it with most meals and it didn't do her any harm as she went on to live for over ninety years.

In the seventeenth century and for around the next 200 years, St Giles' was the base and home for many doctors, who lived in huge Georgian houses. Many of the leading doctors of the Norfolk and Norwich Hospital who lived here went on to become magistrates, mayors and even Sheriff. One in particular, Dr P. Eade, was given the freedom of the city and was knighted by Queen Victoria in 1885. He lived in Churchman House, which is now the Norwich Register Office.

In January 1779, fifty smugglers with horses loaded with tea had been spotted passing through Cringleford tollgate. By the time they reached Norwich, they had split into separate groups and thirty-three entered through St Giles' Gate on their way to Dukes Palace Yard, where they were stopped by excise officers. All but one smuggler and his horse escaped.

The demand for tea was so great it could not be met by the smugglers in the normal way and in the eighteenth century the Revenue were being defrauded of £3,170,233 per annum, a huge sum in those days. To cash in on the bonanza, adulterated tea was sold by unscrupulous dealers, with leaves of ash, elder, sloe, liquorice and other trees, shrubs and plants being added to previously brewed tea leaves. Smugglers passed this on with a severe health risk to the unsuspecting customers. To smuggle and sell this tea was considered a far worse crime than ordinary smuggling and many spent long years in jail. Norwich people petitioned Parliament to express their concern about the amount of adulterated tea sold in the city.

On 10 September 1874, a dentist from St Giles', Mr Richard White, was a passenger in a horrific train crash outside Norwich. Dr Pitt, who attended the scene, gave him brandy on a soaked handkerchief and this kept him alive for three hours until he could be extracted from his position, which he described as 'like being in a coffin upside down'.

In 1884, the Norwich Corporation ordered the Roman Catholic church of St John the Baptist to be pulled down halfway through its construction at St Giles' Gate because its dimensions had been exceeded. The Duke of Norfolk, who was covering all the costs, was most upset. He wrote to the Lord Mayor stating that he would leave the church half built and proceed to build the other half some miles away, where he knew even half a church would be welcomed. Eventually the Corporation gave in and the church was completed in 1910. Norwich Cathedral is built in a valley but St John's is on the highest site in Norwich.

St Gregory's Alley

St Gregory's church is located in this alley, which lies north of Pottergate. The alley runs through an archway below the level of the church altar. A spectacular funeral took place here in 1812. Watched by a crowd of 2,000 people, James Parsons, a farrier employed by veterinary surgeon Richard Watson, was buried with full 'veterinary and masonic' ceremonies. There were two farriers in white aprons, with their implements bound with white ribbons and reversed. Six brethren of Stags Lodge in their full regalia carried the corpse and a sword, his masonic apron and collar were laid on the pall. Parsons' favourite horse was covered in black velvet. The headstall and bridle were adorned with white roses and facings, emphasising that he was a bachelor. A moving dirge sung by all those present gave everyone much satisfaction that their brother and fellow craftsman had earned so much respect.

St Helen's Square

Adjoining Bishopsgate, this square is a place of peaceful tranquillity in an otherwise busy city, an oasis of grass and flowers. There are quiet almshouses within the shadow of the church of St Helen that now forms part the Great Hospital (see Bishopsgate), which was founded in 1249 by Bishop Suffield. In the grounds is an old cannon that dates back to Kett's Rebellion. It is a constant reminder that nearby Bishopsgate witnessed harrowing scenes when wounded and dying men were dragged down to the river to be drowned.

St John's Alley

This alley is best approached from Pottergate, under the arch of St John's church. Halfway down is the Maddermarket Theatre, formerly a Roman Catholic chapel and a warehouse. It is the home of the Norwich Players, founded by Walter Nugent Monck. Monck rented a beautiful house in the area for forty years, eventually owning it, and here he entertained many friends and actors. Their first theatre was a Music House, holding just under 100 people. After the First World War, they found a permanent home in the chapel, which had been turned into a baking powder factory and later became a Salvation Army citadel. Monk raised £3,000 from supporters and converted its interior into a copy of a Shakespearean theatre. He had that indefineable star quality, was a dictator on stage but had a good sense of humour, always getting respect and willing obedience from the performers. His name will live on forever at this theatre, as will a ghost that Monk first saw leaving a confessional box that had been left at the side of the stage. This friendly apparition is said to be a priest or monk who wants to celebrate communion with everyone there. It has been seen many times by actors, stagehands, and even members of the audience, one of whom saw it move across the stage during a play. The productions are of the highest standard and, in keeping with tradition, the actors prefer to remain anonymous, as does the ghost.

Below left: *The theatre can be reached through the arches near the church of St John Maddermarket.*

Below right: *The attractive entrance to the cosy Maddermarket Theatre.*

St John Maddermarket

This name is taken from madder, *rubia tinctorum*, a plant grown in Norfolk that produced a red dye used in the medieval textile industry based in this area. At one time, the street was known as St John's Street.

There is an excellent display of brasses, said to be the finest in Norwich, in the nearby church of St John Maddermarket. They commemorate the family of John Terry, who was mayor in 1523, plus other mayors and leading citizens such as Leonard Sotherton, whose home is now the Strangers' Hall museum. The wall of the churchyard was knocked down and rebuilt in 1578 to allow the road to be widened so that the carriage of Queen Elizabeth I could safely pass through on her way to the Bishop's Palace. She stayed in the city for six days and there was much pageantry and entertainment.

The Duke of Norfolk's Palace was at the end of the alley, where it meets St Andrew's Street. Hemmed in by buildings on both sides, it was not an ideal place and its grounds extended to the banks of the River Wensum, which was heavily polluted. On many occasions when guests were brought here by boat, they complained that it smelt like a sewer. In St John's church, there is a memorial to the Duke's second wife, Lady Margaret, dated 1791. It was at the palace that the Duke planned to marry Mary, Queen of Scots and thereby rule over England. This was a big mistake and the Duke was beheaded at the Tower of London.

This area was a base for the unemployed young people of Norwich to meet and find jobs. Local tradesmen and management from stately homes wishing to hire staff came here to select suitable applicants. Even John Crome found work here in 1781, when he was thirteen years old.

There is an excellent morris dancing group in Norwich called Kemp's men. They have taken their name from the most famous Morris dancer of all time, Will Kemp. He was an actor friend of Shakespeare, who was always willing to take on a bet. In 1599, after a small row over who was the public's favourite, a wager at odds of 3-1 was made that Kemp would morris dance from London to Norwich. This feat was to take place in the winter, on roads that were basically tracks full of potholes. It took him four weeks in ghastly weather, with nine days of actual dancing and the remainder as rest days. He enjoyed royal hospitality en route and was entertained with all sorts of distractions, including money that was thrown to him by well-wishers. At Stratford Langton, bear-baiting was laid on and although he enjoyed this form of spectacle he couldn't get through the crowds to see it, so growling was heard from Kemp as well as the bear. By the time he reached Chelmsford, he had at least 200 supporters with him.

He was not adverse to dancing with the ladies; he danced for nearly an hour with a young girl in Chelmsford, and in Sudbury with a well-endowed women with 'sides well larded and every bone with fat flesh guarded', who had bells strapped to her ample legs. She was huge but had the stamina to dance with him to Melford and Kemp was so impressed that he paid for her to drink 'a skinful' for the rest of the day. On his arrival in Norwich, he was advised by the mayor to delay the finish of his walk for a few days until the Saturday. Having already entered the city by St Giles' Gate, he re-entered through St Stephen's Gate on the Saturday and danced to the marketplace. As he was dancing, an attractive girl came too close and his toe somehow got caught in her loosely tied petticoat. It came down and was picked up by some local lads who started to tease her, causing her to go scarlet with embarrassment.

Kemp was formally greeted by the mayor, Roger Weld, who then led the way to the churchyard of St John Maddermarket. Will completed his dancing by leaping over the churchyard wall. The mayor provided a civic lunch and procession to Market Place, where he gave Will £5 as a present, plus 40s a year and the honour of being made a freeman of the merchant venturers. In return, Will gave him his dancing shoes, called buskins and the mayor nailed these to the guildhall to show the height of Kemp's leap.

Kemp is buried in Southwark and on his gravestone are the words: 'Welcome from Norwich, Kempe all joy to see, Thy safe return from morriscoed lustily'.

St Julian's Alley

A small group of officials, including a surgeon, gathered in the churchyard of St Julian's at dawn on 17 June 1817. They were opening up the grave of a poor woman who had died of smallpox and had been buried two days previously. Screams and banging noises had been heard emanating from her grave and it was suspected that she had been buried alive. There was no doubt that she was dead when the coffin was opened but it was never certain whether she was dead when she was buried. The official findings were 'inconclusive'.

St Martin's Lane

The Inner Ring Road took its toll here, as parts of the original lane were lost due to its construction. There used to be tanneries here, which by their nature produced nasty smells, hence the lane became known as Dirty Lane or Filthy Lane but happily these unpleasant names have faded into obscurity. The nicest part of this street is the church and a few old flint cottages that have been well renovated.

St Martin at Oak Wall Lane

William Sheward, landlord of the Key and Castle Inn, was staying with his sister during New Year celebrations in 1851 when, having indulged in rather too much alcohol, his conscience got the better of him and he decided to confess to a crime that he had committed eighteen years previously, when he was running a business as a tailor in Tabernacle Street. He was lazy, shiftless and hard drinking so the business never made money. His wife nagged him from dawn to dusk, so one day, in a fit of rage, he stabbed her to death with a pair of tailoring shears. He told everyone that she had left him and nobody connected her disappearance with the mysterious body parts that later appeared around the city and also in some local villages. The poor lady had a fine head of long hair, which Sherward cut off and cast around as he walked through Norwich; her trimmed head was never found. He married again in 1862 and worked as a pawnbroker on King Street, prior to becoming a landlord. When he had sobered up at his sister's house, he tried to retract but she reported him to the police. At his trial he was convicted and sentenced to death. On 20 June 1869, he became one of the few criminals to be executed on the roof of the Norwich City Gaol outside St Giles' Gate.

St Martin at Palace Plain

This area was once known as a compound called Bitch Hill, which became Whores Lane in the late eighteenth century. However, the name Bitch Hill did not arise because ladies of the night traded here but was merely derived from 'beech' or 'beak' because of the shape of the land.

It is thought that, in early days, merchant ships berthed on the south side of the river near to the site of St Martin's church. Their cargo was unloaded onto a gravel terrace called a 'bychel', a large open area which was considerably more attractive in the Georgian period. A number of Robert Kett's men are buried in this church, which is near to where Lord Sheffield was killed. Sir Thomas Erpingham, who was in charge of the English archers at the Battle of Agincourt and was featured in the writings of Shakespeare, lived in a house on the east side of the church. It was demolished and a gasworks built in its place but thankfully that too has gone.

1811 saw a charming funeral for popular lamplighter John Thompson, who died at the age of sixty-two, 'his lamp of light being out and his oil consumed'. He was buried at night and his cortège was accompanied by all his fellow workers with their ladders and lit torches. They illuminated his last journey home in front of thousands of people assembled in St Martin at Palace Plain.

There are some excellent buildings on the north side of this street, including one that was a Drawing and Watercolour School of Painting, opened in 1824 by a famous Norwich artist called John Sell Cotman. Totally original in style, he was considered second only to Turner for his watercolours. He lived in this house for ten years, until his extravagant lifestyle finally put him

A visit by the Prince of Wales in the 1920s.

This tall building was the home of artist John Sell Cotman until his lavish lifestyle drained all his resources.

into debt and he was evicted.

Next door to Bussey's Garage is the Wig and Pen, once known as the White Lion, one of six inns of this name that once existed in the city. The name of this one was changed because solicitors and barristers from the nearby law courts meet here for refreshment. The Wig and Pen has two small shields on its façade that date back to the sixteenth century; they have never been identified.

St Mary's Plain

Here we have yet another Norwich church that has been converted into something far removed from its original purpose: St Mary's church is now a craft centre. The main part of the church dates back to 1477 and its round flint tower is probably the oldest in East Anglia. This parish had a dreadful reputation for being a slum, full of noxious courts and alleys. However, it did have associations with the Norwich school of painters. John Sell Cotman was baptised in the church, and both John Crome and Robert Ladbrooke had their weddings here. Also, Luke Hansard lived nearby while serving his printing apprenticeship. At one time, there were plans to turn the church into a theatre named after Hansard but they fell through.

St Peter's Street

This street, which runs in front of City Hall, was once known as Overrowe because it was the highest row of the market. Old Crome described it has having a complexion 'like Brown Windsor soup'. It is difficult to imagine this road as it once was, surrounded by a mass of courtyards and alleys containing houses, shops of every description, inns and even the city police detectives. Important though they all were, everything had to go to make way for City Hall, the new headquarters of the city's civic leaders. They had been working in various buildings scattered around this area, including the ancient guildhall. The new City Hall was opened by King George VI on 29 October 1938.

This award-winning structure received a mixed reaction from the public, some of whom called it a 'factory'. However, the front doors are interesting: made of bronze and designed by A. Hardman, they show the history of various industries and significant events that happened in Norwich and there is also a large relief of lions. The high tower with its clock and bells can been seen and heard from two to three miles outside the city. However, its clock is not as attractive as that on the end of the guildhall. During the Second World War, the tower proved very useful as a lookout tower and was a base for air-raid warning signals.

Opposite City Hall is the St Peter Mancroft church, whose name is said to derive from 'magna crofta', meaning big croft or meadow. The church has an attractive 100ft tower and a spire that takes it to 146ft, making it the largest and finest church in Norwich. An absolute treasure, it was built in the fifteenth century and restored in Victorian times. It has 'pepperpot' turrets and spirelet and a fine peal of twelve bells, which is frequently heard on the local radio station. The bells are often rung on Tuesdays and many visitors and tourists leave Norwich with unforgettable memories of its music.

There are so many things worth mentioning about this church, not least its stained glass. The east window contains fragments of glass that were saved from an explosion that destroyed nearly all the church windows. As a result of the uprisings that took place in the city during the Civil

The largest and finest church in Norwich is St Peter Mancroft.

War in the seventeenth century, a huge explosion occurred in the Committee House, which was later the site of the Bethel Hospital. Nearly 100 barrels of gunpowder blew up, killing and injuring many people. This and other buildings were destroyed, and glass was smashed in all the surrounding properties of Market Place, especially St Peter Mancroft's and St Stephen's churches. Local mason Marin Morley was paid £55, a huge amount in those days, to repair the tracery of the east window.

The church is filled with beautiful stone and woodwork, bow chests, brasses and paintings, including one old picture of a toad-like devil piercing St Paul's leg. In 1349, when the Black Death attacked Norwich and killed two-fifths of the population, the churchyard of St Peter Mancroft was enlarged to accommodate the remains of the plague victims. Half the priests in the city caught the illness and died because they came into contact with many of the victims when helping them.

A horse dealer who lived in St Peter Mancroft set up home with a woman from Kent who had left her husband. The husband traced her but she wouldn't go back with him. The horse dealer offered to buy the lady for £5 and the husband agreed. The horse dealer placed a halter around her neck and on 9 February 1805 the husband took her to the marketplace and publicly surrendered all right and title to her for the princely sum.

More recently, there were macabre happenings in this street. A city police inspector called in at the police station office, where the constable on duty laughingly said he had just thrown a murderer out of the station. The man said that he had chopped up a number of his relatives but, because he smelled of alcohol, the constable had dismissed him as an attention-seeker. The inspector found the man in St Peter Street, took him back to the station and organised a check on his address. A scene of carnage was discovered and the man was formally invited to remain at the station.

St Saviour's Lane

The lane connects Magdalen Street with Blackfriars Street, the old Rotten Row. It passes along the south side of St Saviour's church, which is now used as a youth arts centre. St Saviour's Alley runs around the church from Magdalen Street to St Saviour's Lane.

Mathew Parker (1504-75), who became Archbishop of Canterbury in 1559, was born in this parish and educated in the parish of St Clement.

St Stephen's Street

Starting from where St Stephen's Road enters the city at St Stephen's Gate, this is the principal route into the city from the south. The name is taken from the parish church in Rampant Horse Street, which was the name of the original St Stephen's Street. From the seventeenth century, this street was known as Tuns Corner, from an inn called the Three Tunnes.

On 17 June 1779, a gang of smugglers with twenty horses loaded with tea passed through St

This junction became known as Buntings Corner after the drapery store on the right.

Stephen's Gate at two o'clock in the morning. The militia on guard spotted them and gave chase along St Stephen's Street, ending up at Chapel Field. Having dismounted, the smugglers ran off. They left their horses with the 'dollops', which was the name given to bags or sacks of tea of different weights. A week later, the Court of Mayoralty dismissed the gatekeeper for letting the smugglers into the city.

On 3 February 1823 the City of Norwich public house had to be reconstructed after a floor fell through in an adjoining function room, where a noisy 'Ranters' religious meeting was taking place. Over 125 participants were packed into the room and they crashed through the ceiling. Twenty-five injured were taken to the Norfolk and Norwich Hospital and one man had to have his leg amputated.

In later years, part of this street was popularly known as Buntings Corner, from Bunting's Drapery Store. It was housed in a building designed by architect A.F. Scott but the upper floors and attic were destroyed in a Second World War air raid. The store is now Marks & Spencer.

Another shop in the street was the Co-op. One night the electricity failed and the manager pronounced the loss of all refrigerated products. They would be perfectly all right for some time but he would not be allowed to sell them. He asked the attending police officer if he would like to take some away and, in the next hour, mobile units, CID, sergeants, inspectors and adjoining beat constables arrived at the shop. The manager soon found that he did not have a disposal problem.

A number of fine Edwardian buildings can still be seen in this street, although they may have been hidden away somewhat. A good example is the Burlington Building, designed in 1904 by J. Owen Bond, which is now hidden behind Debenhams. It is worth taking the time to study the building because it has a façade of imitation balconies, covered with some rather disinterested goddesses.

St Stephen's Street is currently undergoing major reconstruction, especially at the crossroads with Westlegate, and both roads are under review for traffic and pedestrian flow. The council are said to be consulting with the public for their views on any proposed changes.

St Swithin's Road

Just inside the city walls opposite Dereham Road, this road runs to Westwick Street. There is also a St Swithin's Alley, which is a passage from St Benedict's Street to Westwick Street alongside St Swithin's church. In this alley is Hampshire Hog Yard, the site of the Hampshire Hog public house.

Southgate Lane

This is a long and twisting route from the top of Bracondale to King Street. It contains the remains of the church of St Peter Southgate, from which the street took its name. The church at the south end of King Street was demolished in 1887, and only a small part of the tower remains. There used to be a cottage at the top of the hill which was occupied by an official who kept his eye on the ships moored at Carrow.

Surrey Street

Surrey House, the home of the Earl of Surrey, gave its name to the street, which is now well known as the location of the headquarters of Norwich Union. This fine building was George Skipper's most famous work and has a magnificent marble hall and boardroom. The marble was meant for Westminster Cathedral but was not prepared in time, so George convinced his clients to buy it.

Sir James Edward Smith had a substantial house here. He was an admirer of outstanding Swedish botanist Carl Linnaeus, who was a friend of Sir Joseph Banks, Captain Cook's botanist. When Linnaeus died, Wolseley managed to buy his library and artefacts for £1,000, which he had borrowed from his parents. The items were shipped over from Sweden and during the voyage a boat approached, which tried to intercept and take the collection on behalf of the King of Sweden, who was on board, but it was foiled. When the Linnaean Society was formed in 1788, Smith returned to the city. Norwich is known as the City of Gardens; this reputation was gained because the Flemish weavers were first-class gardeners. At his house in Surrey Street, Smith taught botany and zoology and became a highly respected member of Norwich society. He was also a musician and composed hymns for the Baptist church of the Octagon chapel. There is a plaque at the rear of the Sir Garnet Wolseley public house in Market Place, denoting his birthplace.

William Tuffs of Surrey Street was taken to court in 1881, aged ten. He had fallen in with a bad crowd and had stolen 2s 6d and some important slides from Dr Roche. After being found guilty, he was sent to Ardwicke Green Industrial School until he reached the age of sixteen.

At the corner of Surrey Street and All Saints Green is a house that most readers will have no problem in identifying. It was the home of the BBC and was designed by architect Thomas Ivory (1709-1779), who was also responsible for another property on the opposite side of the road, at the junction with Bull Lane. This was built in 1771 and is named Ivory House. It became the militia barracks in 1860 and has been recently restored. Thomas Ivory also designed the Octagon chapel, the Assembly House and Norwich Theatre.

The thatched Boar's Head public house, on the corner of Surrey Street.

There used to be a very old thatched inn on the corner of Surrey Street and St Stephen's Street named the Boar's Head. This received a direct hit from an incendiary bomb during the Second World War. As the fire brigade were experiencing a water shortage because much of the city was on fire from the bombing raids, this unfortunate inn burned to the ground.

The bus station was an eyesore in this street but is now being demolished to make way for a modern facility that should do more justice to this fine city.

Swan Lane

A small medieval lane taking its name from an old inn, Swan Lane connects London Street to Bedford Street. There is a fine swan on the sign over Dipples jeweller's. The Swan Inn was at one time run by Jem Mace, who was a bare-knuckle fighter as well as a landlord. Mace was born in Beeston, near Dereham. With gypsy blood in his veins and a father who was a blacksmith, plus the build of a weightlifter and rugby player combined, there is no doubt that his strength would mould his future. After working in the forge and then as a sawyer, he would unwind in the local pubs and the evening would often turn into a brawl that Jem always won. On one rare occasion 'Licker' Pratt beat him. He kept the Hampshire Hog in St Benedict's Street. He later moved south and took over a London pub, and to supplement his income he did boxing tours and exhibition matches and finally became world champion in 1862, after forty-three bruising rounds against a fighter named King. He then travelled the world and, when he finally gave up boxing, he used his money to buy pubs and amusement parks. However, business acumen was not his forte and most of the ventures failed. Forced to work again as a boxing coach and give exhibition bouts, he carried on right up to his death at the age of seventy-nine.

T

Ten Bells Lane – Ten Bells Court

This cobbled lane was once known as Hollegate because rainwater rushing down from Cow Hill had washed the lane hollow. For a time it was called St Swithin's, then it changed to Ten Bells Lane after an eighteenth-century pub named the Ten Bells in nearby St Benedict's Street, from where it has been suggested that at one time the bells of ten churches could be plainly heard.

Ten Bells Lane runs into Willets Court and then joins Pottergate. Opposite where they meet is Ten Bells Court, a group of modern houses and flats surrounding St Benedict's Tower, which is nicely preserved on an area of open lawn.

Theatre Street

Originally this was Chapel Field Lane, named after the thirteenth-century chapel of the College of St-Mary-in-the-Fields, which occupied the site where the theatre and the Assembly House now stand. At one time it was regarded as part of Horsemarket, now called Rampant Horse Street. Trams ran through here, outward-bound only, for every morning the street would be jammed with vehicles delivering goods to the market.

There was a fine theatre here built by Thomas Ivory as early as 1757; the actors had previously met in an inn called the White Swan in nearby St Peter's Street. The theatre was replaced by another classical structure, which opened on Easter Monday 27 March 1826 with a saucy selection: *The School for Scandal* and *Youth, Love and Folly or The Female Jockey*. These attracted a different audience to that which the theatre had been become used to. The audiences now were loud in the responses, especially after taking refreshment during the interval, and, on one occasion, an usherette who was selling refreshments was assaulted because she was serving too slow.

This second theatre lasted until Friday 22 June 1934, when it was destroyed by fire. There was a strong wind blowing that day which funnelled through the front doors to the rear as though bellows were being pumped. There was little the fireman could do and everyone working there lost all their possessions, including the band's instruments. Occupying the same site, the present and third theatre was built. It opened on 30 September 1935 with a popular musical called *White Horse Inn*. Later on, when trade plummeted, there were plans to turn it into a bingo hall like many other theatres and cinemas. Thankfully, it was rescued by the city council, who took advice from Laurence Hill and Dick Condon, and between them they turned it into the current successful Civic Theatre.

Norwich Central Library once stood here. Considered by many as a modern and ugly box design, especially as it was surrounded by classical architecture. Unfortunately it burned down on 1 August 1994 and a huge number of priceless books, documents and artefacts were lost forever. During excavations after the fire, a Viking gold ingot – the only one ever found in Britain – was discovered. The first-class traditions of the city library service have been continued in the new

Millennium Library based in the Forum, which was opened by the Queen on 18 July 2002. Although modern in appearance, it has fitted in nicely and has become a tourist attraction.

The Assembly House is set back from the road in its own courtyard, on a site that was occupied by the chapel and hospice of St-Mary-in-the-Field, founded in 1248. It is a wonderful design of domestic architecture that has seen many changes and additions to the original structure. In 1754, John Hobart leased the house to a small number of leading Norwich citizens and aldermen for 500 years and since then it has had a mixed career. For over a century, it was an exclusive place of entertainment and recreation for the gentry. There was a large ballroom lit by ten chandeliers, which was the venue for a fabulous ball on 21 December 1805. The ball was held to celebrate the victory at the Battle of Trafalgar and went on until dawn the following day. Famous composers including Lizst played in the house and Madame Tussaud showed her exhibition here before she had her own building in London. For twenty-one years it was the headquarters of the Norwich Freemasons, before they moved to St Giles in 1876. From the nineteenth century until 1933, it was the Norwich High School for Girls.

The building was used as a warehouse and then the headquarters of the Army Camouflage School during the Second World War. It escaped damage during the war but it did have a close shave in September 1940, when a huge delayed-action bomb landed in the street. The area was cleared for five days until the bomb was eventually disarmed by the army disposal squad. In 1950, a generous local businessman named H.J. Sexton presented the building to the city as an arts centre. There is a small film theatre in the west wing called the Noverre Cinema after Victorian dancing master Frank Noverre. There was a serious fire in 1994, which caused a large amount of damage that took three years to rectify. It now has a pleasant restaurant and is an oasis of peaceful tranquillity, and a meeting point for many different groups.

Below: *The entrance of the attractive theatre, which is said to be haunted.*

Right: *The stately interior of the Assembly House.*

Thorn Lane

Running downhill from Ber Street to Rouen Road, the lane's early name was Sandgate, probably referring to its original sand surface. The current name comes from the St-Michael-at-Thorn church, which was unfortunately destroyed during the Second World War, although the original thorn tree kept growing in isolation for a number of years. All that can be seen of the church now is a wall plaque marking the site.

The church's gruesome history is worth recording. Its graveyard was full of those who died in the castle by some terrible methods, such as Myles Kilvert, a felon who was stripped naked, tied to the ground and pressed to death by heavy weights; Mary Adams, who was executed for burning an outhouse to the ground and Bill Bales, who was hanged for stabbing a horse to death. They were buried on top of 245 plague victims.

Three Kings Lane

Like a number of Norwich streets in the 1900s, Three Kings Lane took its name from a public house off Upper Westwick Street. Before this, it was known as St Margaret's Lane from the church in Lower Westwick Street which has a brass to Anne Rede, dated 1567, and a fourteenth-century chest. It was originally Backhouse Lane and, during excavations in the 1970s, remains of a bakery were found.

Timberhill

The Second World War and city council planners have failed to devastate this street, which contains buildings characteristic of Norwich. It runs uphill from Orford Hill to Ber Street and its name refers to an open space in front of the church where wood was sold. Prior to the thirteenth century, it was named Durnedale, which is perhaps a description for a 'hidden dale'. There are interesting properties in Palmers Yard and Lion and Castle Yard on the west side of the street, plus a Baptist chapel that was a Georgian warehouse and factory prior to 1833.

At the top of Timberhill, opposite the John Lewis store, is the church of St John the Baptist. It had the ancient title of St John before the Castle Gates, thought to have come from its original purpose in around 1070 to serve the population who were displaced by the building of the castle. This work caused a third of Saxon Norwich to be demolished. The interior contains many attractive paintings and carvings. There is an oil painting of the Mocking of Christ in the style of Van Dyck, a rood beam carved in Oberammergau and a German-made alter reredos.

Peter the Wild Boy of Timberhill was born in the Forest of Herenhausen. He was found by King George I on a hunting expedition and brought back to England as a curiosity. The King took him under his wing and ensured that he was looked after. However, he proved impossible to educate properly and his wild nature took hold, so he escaped into the countryside. In time he found his way into Norwich, where he was captured and sent to prison as a tramp. He was eventually returned to his original keeper after a fire destroyed the prison in 1751, and he went on to live until he was seventy-three.

Tombland

This place at the western entrance of the Cathedral Close was the Civic Centre and original market place of Anglo-Saxon Norwich. Its situation suggests that the name derives from 'thum' or 'tomb, meaning open space. Norwich residents fiercely defended their rights to use this space, especially against the early monks of the cathedral. Fairs were held here at Easter and Christmas, and markets throughout the year. However it did become cluttered with semi-permanent stalls after the Second World War. These were taken down in the late 1960s after a furious legal battle, which the council lost. The area has now improved, with an open aspect revealing fine buildings and the medieval cathedral gates, and any further building has been banned. The Erpingham Gateway into the cathedral dates from 1420. It was erected to the memory of Sir Thomas Erpingham, a warrior at the Battle of Agincourt, and there is a statue of him in a niche above the archway.

An important resident of Tombland was Augustine Steward, who was three times mayor, a highly respected figure and an MP. During Kett's Rebellion, his house became the headquarters of Italian mercenaries under Lord Northampton. They were unsuccessful in battle and later the house was raided and he was robbed. With great risk to himself, Steward managed to escape and unlock St Benedict's Gate, letting in the Earl of Warwick with his army of German mercenaries. With their help, the rebellion was crushed. The house is quite tilted and unusually attractive; it is currently the office of the Tourist Board.

The fifteenth-century church of St George Tombland is of interest as it is one of only three in the city retaining some Georgian furnishings. It has a seventeenth-century font cover with a statuette of St George and the dragon, and a memorial to the mayor of Norwich in 1611, Thomas Anguish. He was a freeman of the city and Sheriff, and when he died he left provision in his will for a poor school. This was built in Fishergate in 1618 and operated until 1885.

A huge riot took place in Norwich during 1766. In this street, a mob protesting against the scarcity and high prices of corn and provisions totally destroyed a baker's shop, one of many of this trade in the city that suffered the same fate. The mob also destroyed the homes of the bakers and many new mills that had been built. It took the authorities many hours to quell the riot and thirty of the ringleaders were tried by special commission on 1 December 1766. Eight were given death sentences but only two were carried out, on 10 January 1767, to set an example to the others.

At the point where Tombland meets Wensum Street is an ancient building protected by huge statues of Samson and Hercules. They would dwarf the burly bouncers of this once-popular ballroom and concert hall for the young and lively of Norwich. On one occasion, two plain-clothes police officers on a nightshift beat spotted an open window. Suspecting intruders, they entered through the window and were mistaken for intruders themselves by three public-spirited citizens, who were passing by at the time. After thoroughly checking the ballroom and finding everything in order, the two officers could not resist the temptation of trying the various instruments left on the bandstand. The cacophony produced was far removed from any form of music. It subsequently turned out that the public-spirited citizens had rushed to a telephone and dialled 999. The impromptu concert was short-lived because the ballroom was suddenly full of

Above left and right: *Statues of Samson and Hercules on an ancient building, where Tombland meets Wensum Street.*

uniforms and they were both arrested. They were quickly identified as police officers on patrol and released, red faced, after a critical comment from the duty sergeant about their actions, both on and off the stage.

U

Unthank Road

This modern road was once a drive over land belonging to Colonel Unthank. In the fourteenth century 'unthank' meant land settled on without permission. Unthank is also a well-known northen surname. Near to St John's Cathedral is the site of the guildhall of 1407. This was notorious for the prisons on its ground floor and vaults. There was a small treadmill on which every prisoner had to work; their number was called out at the whim of the duty warder. Each inmate would do a stint of fifteen minutes with a five-minute break on three-hour shifts. Lunchbreak was one hour, during which time they built their strength up with a hard-baked meal of maize and oatmeal. Then it was back to work until they went to bed.

Henry Cross-Grove lived and worked here in 1706. He was an Irishman of wild outspoken character. Editor of the *Norwich Gazette*, he was a highly intelligent eccentric who enjoyed many a stormy written battle against politicians. Plays with dubious language were attacked, as were the audiences who he called raging 'nuts'. He was the first of what today would be called an agony aunt, answering all letters addressed to the editor on whatever subject was brought up. He would of course be quite barbed in his responses. The establishment once took him to court for treason and he was greatly looking forward to verbal exchanges but the case was weak and was thrown out, much to his annoyance. When his long-suffering wife passed away, he buried her at the ungodly hour of 11 p.m. The *Gazette* had a spectacular front page the next day, consisting of Father Time, hourglasses, skeletons, coffins and winding sheets as well as a eulogy. Henry Cross-Grove continued to fight on for thirty-six years at the *Norwich Gazette*, which he finally owned. In 1824 the city prison was built here and lasted until 1900 when it was replaced by a new building on Mousehold.

Upper and Lower Goat Lane

These streets run parallel to each other. Upper Goat Lane was known in the thirteenth century as Stonegate, derived from 'stongate' meaning 'stony street', as Norwich streets were not paved until the fifteenth century. It became Stonegate Magna and contained a market selling stoneware manufactured in potteries located in Pottergate. Goat Lane is taken from an inn that once stood in Upper Goat Lane; it even had a landlord of the same name, Charlie Goat!

There are two well-known buildings here that have survived the ravages of war and planners. Near City Hall is a kitchen design business called Fired Earth, housed in an Edwardian building designed by George Skipper, and at the other end is the Friends Meeting House designed by John Patience. The area still has individual character, with many small interesting shops, and was a favourite place for relaxation for showbusiness artists appearing at music halls in the vicinity. Even now, office workers and shoppers take their lunchbreaks on the seats lining the pavements, weather permitting.

W

Waterside

Cow Tower can be seen from here, which is where the monks collected their dues from boats or ships travelling upriver.

Weavers Lane

Country linen weavers lived here and used this street to sell their wares on stalls every Saturday.

Wellington Lane

This road is just inside the old city wall, parts of which have been preserved, and runs north between the original site of St Giles' Gate and the site of St Benedict's Gate. The name is taken from the Wellington tavern, which in 1647 stood close by the old wall off Upper St Giles Street.

The portion of this lane north of Pottergate used to be a separate street called Duck Lane, no doubt after another pub.

Wensum Street

This street is sometimes considered to be part of Fye Bridge Street. In the eighteenth century, it was named Cook Street, derived from 'coquinaria', which loosely translates to 'the office of cook'. The city cooks lived here and once it even became known as Cookerowe.

At the junction with Palace Street, Wensum Street and Tombland is the famous Maid's Head Hotel, a very old and historic establishment going back to the thirteenth century. It was the original Bishop's Palace, owned by Herbert de Losinga, and a local story is that after it became an inn, Edward the Black Prince stayed there in 1350. The name was changed to the Mayd's Hedde in the fourteenth century, when it was described in the Paston Letters. Its Georgian front is depicted on some ancient prints of the period and it now has Edwardian mock-Tudor façades.

Thomas Anguish was born in 1538 and was mayor in 1611. At a reception in his honour, there was a firework display that went wrong and in the ensuing panic over thirty people were crushed to death. Opposite the Maid's Head is Samson and Hercules House, with its huge statues of those heroes (*see* Tombland). This old building is on the original site of a house owned by the Duchess of Suffolk. The current seventeenth-century building has been altered several times. It will always be known as a ballroom and dance hall, especially during the Second World War, when it was a popular spot for our own troops as well as the American forces. Even before the war, it was well loved as a dance hall for nearly 100 years.

Next door is Augustine Steward House, named after the sixteenth-century mayor of Norwich. In the fifteenth century, this was the headquarters of two mercenary armies sent to quell Kett's Rebellion.

Westlegate

Once a tiny road with attractive small gabled houses, it was only possible for fairly small horse-drawn vehicles to negotiate this road. It probably takes its name from 'wastel', an early form of pastry. The road is overlooked by the fine tower of All Saints' church, one of many that gave the city the title of the City of Churches. This area suffered badly at the time of the Black Death in the fourteenth century and most of its population perished.

The road is now regarded as an extension of All Saints Green, leading to St Stephen's. Had road widening and modernisation not taken place in 1925, a few of the early cottages on the north side would have fallen down. Popular family firms such as Deacon's fish and chip restaurant on the corner of Red Lion Street disappeared, although Joy's wet fish business on the opposite side of the road survived until 1936 when their lease ran out. It was not renewed by Norwich Union, who had an office entrance in the street and were desperate to expand their business. The entrance had a pair of magnificent iron gates that had seen use in London 100 years earlier.

A nineteenth-century lantern slide of the Barking Dickey Inn.

Next door to the unaltered sixteenth-century church of All Saints was a popular public house called the Barking Dickey, later to become a greengrocer's and then a café. A small alley took its name from the pub. 'Dickey' is an old Norfolk expression for a donkey. It remains a mystery as to where 'Barking' came from, though it is said to be based on a comment made by a local, who said that the creature on the sign above the pub when it was called the Light Horseman looked like 'a cross between a dog and a donkey'.

Westwick Street

Recalling the name of one of the first settlements out of which the city of Norwich was formed, the street is based on the old quarter called Wymer or Westwick, that ran from Charing Cross to the Inner Ring Road at Heigham Street. Here there was a gate called Hell Gate, an unpopular name that has not survived. The name change may be due to the fact that pilgrims passed by on their way to the Walsingham Shrine; maybe it would have upset them and not furthered their cause. Heading into the city, on the right hand side is St Margaret's Street, named after one of three churches that are within a stone's throw of each other. It has an interesting spandrel in the south porch of the church, depicting St Margaret with a monk.

There was once a large plain north of the church but this has virtually disappeared; what little remains of it is now a playground for young children. Part of the street was once known as Letestere Row, meaning Listers' or Dyers' Row. Due to its proximity to the River Wensum, many weavers and dyers lived and worked here, using the water to clean and dye their materials, which at the same time heavily polluted the river. The area is prone to flooding and during the great deluge of 1912, the whole area was under water.

Bullards and Sons' Anchor Brewery building is still here and has been converted into apartments. At one time it was one of the offices of the Municipal Insurance Group. The Adam

And Eve in Upper Westwick Street was thought to be the oldest pub in Norwich; it is now part of the premises of Cooke's, the musical instrument retailer. The landlord in the early 1800s was Fiddy Barnes, who perpetuated stories that the pub was haunted by several ghosts, including the most respected one, Lord Sheffield. During Kett's Rebellion, this man had his head nearly chopped off by Fulke the butcher. The lord's staff carried the poor man's body into the Adam and Eve, where he died on a table. Even now, customers claim to have felt cold draughts pass by them, and at the same time tankards have been seen swinging on hooks, when all the doors to the bars have been shut.

Whitefriars

The bridge that carries this road over the river is on the site of the oldest recorded bridge in Norwich, going back to the thirteenth century. Some historians argue that there was a crossing here before the Norman Conquest and there is a possibility that there was a wooden bridge called St Martin's here at the beginning of the eleventh century. The name of the road is taken from the Carmelites or White Friars who had an establishment on the riverside. Jarrold's the printers have their factory on the original site of the friary and they have taken the trouble to preserve the Friars' medieval crypt as a museum of printing. The road is now a major route into the city from the north of the county.

Whitefriars, the oldest recorded bridge still standing in Norwich.

White Lion Street

In the Middle Ages, this was called Saddelgate, where most of the manufacturing and selling of saddles, bridles, bits and spurs took place. The name changed according to which livery trader dominated: it was once Bridlesmiths' Row and then Lorimer's Row, from 'larrimer', meaning harness-maker. In the seventeenth century, it became White Lion Street, from the White Horse Inn that stood in the middle of the north side of the lane. Originally part of the Jewish quarter, it has retained fragments of its early character. There is a side entrance from the street into the Royal Arcade.

Willow Lane

Connecting Cow Hill to St Giles, this lane took its name from the willow trees growing on its south side on waste ground next to the churchyard of St Giles. It was the responsibility of the mayor to ensure that the trees were trimmed and restrained at regular intervals.

Notable author George Burrow had a house at the end of this sloping lane. Another notable man of letters also lived here, Francis Blomefield. Educated at Cambridge, he became rector of Fersfield near Diss and spent most of his life writing a history of Norfolk. Having accepted an invitation to Oxnead House, built by William Paston, he browsed through boxes of ledgers and letters and found the famous Paston Letters. These were a perfect record of life during the Wars of the Roses from the point of view of a middle-class family. Sadly the letters were later stolen by a scoundrel that Blomefield had employed as an engraver. Blomefield carried on and published his first part of the *History of Norfolk*, which was an instant success. His parishioners hardly ever saw him but he continued his other passion, foxhunting. Unfortunately he had difficulty in maintaining his pack of hounds on clergyman's pay and the proceeds of the second volume of his book. He never completed the third volume because on a visit to London he caught smallpox and died at the age of forty-six.

Winkle Row

Mustard manufacturer J. J. Colman owned four cottages here, which were close to the factory. There is no satisfactory reason for the strange name of this street.

Z

Zipfels Court

This is a popular name in Norwich and comes from a famous German family of clockmakers, going back to the late eighteenth century. The dynasty lasted 100 years.

Index of Street Names

Other local titles published by Tempus

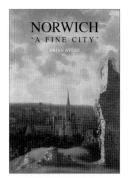

Norwich 'A Fine City'
BRIAN AYERS

Brian Ayers shows how the city of Norwich has developed over the last 1,000 years, highlighting in particular the Norman castle and cathedral, the numerous medieval churches, the importance of Dutch 'Stranger' immigrants for post-medieval prosperity, and the buildings of the great Victorian industries.

0 7524 2549 8

Norwich Speedway
NORMAN JACOBS

Norwich has been one of the most famous and best-loved teams in the history of speedway. From the early days in the 1930s, through the remarkably successful '50s and up to the closure of the promotion in the '60s, this remarkable pictorial history brings the city's rich speedway heritage to life.

0 7524 3152 8

Norwich City Football Club
GARY ENDERBY

Since the foundation of the club in 1902, Norwich City's fortunes have fluctuated dramatically. With nearly 200 illustrations, including player portraits, team groups, action shots, programme covers and cartoons, this book is a comprehensive pictorial history which encompasses the club's 100 year history and is an essential read for anyone with an interest in the Canaries.

0 7524 2266 9

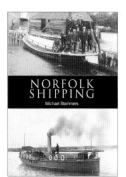

Norfolk Shipping
MICHAEL STAMMERS

The late eighteenth century saw the growth of steam ships and the gradual decline of traditional sailing craft. Norfolk has, though, been a haven for craft such as the fishing vessels that once used the harbour at Great Yarmouth. *Norfolk Shipping* is illustrated with 200 images of just some of the craft that have plied both the North Sea off the coast and inland to the Broads and along the county's main rivers.

0 7524 2757 1

If you are interested in purchasing other books published by Tempus, or in case you have difficulty finding any Tempus books in your local bookshop, you can also place orders directly through our website

www.tempus-publishing.com